UNKNOWN, UNTOLD, AND UNBELIEVABLE STORIES OF
IU
SPORTS

John C. Decker,
Pete DiPrimio, and
Doug Wilson

Indiana University Press

This book is a publication of

Indiana University Press
Office of Scholarly Publishing
Herman B Wells Library 350
1320 East 10th Street
Bloomington, Indiana 47405 USA

iupress.indiana.edu

Manufactured in the United States of America

Library of Congress Cataloging-in-Publication Data

Names: Decker, John C., author. | DiPrimio, Pete, author. |
    Wilson, Doug (Douglas Scott), author.
Title: Unknown, untold, and unbelievable stories of IU
    sports / John C. Decker, Pete DiPrimio, and Doug Wilson.
Description: Bloomington, Indiana : Indiana University
    Press, 2018.
Identifiers: LCCN 2018003211 (print) | LCCN 2018018827
    (ebook) | ISBN 9780253036193 (e-book) | ISBN
    9780253036209 (hardback : alk. paper) | ISBN
    9780253036162 (pbk. : alk. paper)
Subjects: LCSH: Indiana
    University—Sports—History—Anecdotes.
Classification: LCC GV691.I63 (ebook) | LCC GV691.I63 D43
    2018 (print) | DDC 796.04/309772—dc23
LC record available at https://lccn.loc.gov/2018003211

1 2 3 4 5   23 22 21 20 19 18

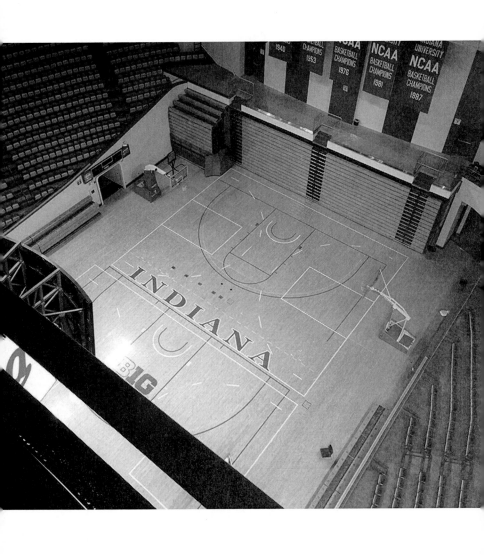

CONTENTS

Acknowledgments

This project couldn't have been completed without the support, aid, and tolerance of a handful of very knowledgeable people and friends at IU Athletics.

IU Assistant Athletic Director Chuck Crabb was not only a primary source for many of the stories but also a source of many great ideas. Chuck's willingness to meet with each of us on numerous occasions over the course of a year is greatly appreciated. He has an encyclopedic knowledge of everything Hoosier-related, and we relied on it heavily. His dedication to IU Athletics is a big reason why so many of the items we wrote about are still around today.

When it comes to anything Indiana football, no one knows more nor is more passionate than former Hoosier player-turned-coach-turned-administrator Mark Deal. Like Chuck, Mark was willing and able to sit down with us on numerous occasions as we defined and refined the stories we wanted to pursue.

IU Associate Athletic Director Jeremy Gray, meanwhile, was a big advocate of this project when it was first pitched over lunch at Nick's, and it couldn't have happened without his support. Not only did Jeremy help us formulize many of the story ideas and point us in the right direction in many instances but he refused to succumb to a fear of heights on the journey to the top of Assembly Hall.

While those three have been key supporters every step of the way, there are countless others that we leaned upon heavily. Several of the stories couldn't have materialized without the aid of men's basketball trainer Tim Garl and assistant athletic director Marty Clark. Former IU media relations director Kit Klingelhoffer was also a willing and reliable source throughout the project. Media Relations staff members Nate Wiechers, Scott Burns, Greg Kincaid, and Jeremy Rosenthal assisted us in tracking down photos that helped tell many of our stories, and Bradley Cook from IU Archives helped immeasurably by giving us access to countless historical items and photos.

Last, but certainly not least, we owe a big thank-you to a handful of people from IU Press. Pam Rude, Dave Miller, Michelle Sybert, Dave Hulsey, Peggy Solic, and Gary Dunham all helped make this a reality. We are especially grateful to our wonderful editor Ashley Runyon, who supported us every step of the way ... even when we seemed to be one step behind in getting done!

UNKNOWN, UNTOLD, AND
UNBELIEVABLE
STORIES OF
IU
SPORTS

Introduction

*Some of the best stories about Indiana University Athletics
have been unknown, untold, or forgotten.*

Until now.

For more than 125 years, Hoosier athletes and coaches have
grabbed headlines with their accomplishments and accolades.
Legendary performers and larger-than-life figures have called
Bloomington home, and their stories have been passed from
one generation to the next.

But for every unforgettable story about a Hoosier athlete,
coach, or program, there's another that's been forgotten. In
some cases, the reason is the passage of time, and in others, it's
because someone didn't want the tale revealed.

But those stories still existed—perhaps in a box tucked deep
in a storage closet in Assembly Hall, or in the recesses of a
long-time employee's mind. They've been waiting to be shared.

In *Unknown, Untold, and Unbelievable Stories of IU Sports,*
we tell many of those unbelievable stories that virtually no one
knows about. From notes kept by Bob Knight on the 1984 US
Olympic Trials to football jerseys worn only once before dis-
appearing, we've uncovered fascinating stories that you didn't
know and might not believe.

How do we know these stories are largely unknown?
Between the three of us, we've written about or for Indiana
University Athletics for more than 70 years. We've liter-
ally penned thousands of articles for outlets including the
*Bloomington Herald Times, Ft. Wayne New Sentinel, Evansville
Courier, Inside Indiana Magazine,* and even Indiana University

Athletics. When anything of significance has happened with Indiana University sports, one of us—if not all three of us—has been there to witness it and report about it for more than 30 years.

Some of these stories we've known, but never told. In other cases, we've heard rumors, and have pieced together the truth. In other instances, we've stumbled into fascinating tales while researching other subjects.

The end results are the following hidden gems about the people, places, and things that have made Indiana University Athletics one of the preeminent athletic programs for more than a century.

We hope that you enjoy the book as much as we loved putting it together. As a journalist, there are few things more enjoyable than telling readers a story they don't know about.

And that's what this book is all about.

1

Men (Temporarily) in Black

John C. Decker

Bloomington's best-known watering hole tells the best-known tales of Indiana University's (IU) storied athletic programs.

Take a seat in a first-floor booth at Nick's English Hut on Bloomington's iconic Kirkwood Avenue and look around. You'll see pictures of championship teams and images of legendary coaches and All-Americans. Wind past the kitchen and up the stairs, and the walls will remind you of the most famous chair ever thrown and of a swimming program that once had no equal.

But make your way to the establishment's newest addition, the second-floor bar, and you'll come across a framed football jersey that's in need of an explanation. Former IU walk-on and current Temple University Athletic Director Pat Kraft's number 47 is encased on the west wall. That jersey was worn in 1997, the first year of former coach Cam Cameron's tenure. That Indiana team went just 2-9 and won only one Big Ten game.

Also of note—Kraft's jersey is black. And basketball Coach Bob Knight hated it.

* * *

When Coach Cam Cameron took over the Indiana football program in 1997, he wanted to make dramatic changes.

The big picture for the former Hoosier quarterback turned NFL assistant coach was trying to find a winning formula for a program that had been mostly losing for generations. In its 110 years of existence, IU football had produced only two Big Ten titles—and one (1945) came before the league even bore its current name.

Recent times weren't much better. After a run of some of the program's greatest successes under Coach Bill Mallory from 1986 to 1993 (six bowl games in eight years), IU football stumbled and sank to some its greatest depths, losing 15 of 16 Big Ten games and 17 of 22 overall from 1995 to 1996.

UNKNOWN, UNTOLD, AND UNBELIEVABLE!

That prompted a coaching change, and Indiana turned to the thirty-six-year-old Cameron. A 1983 Indiana University graduate who played both football and basketball, Cameron had developed a reputation as one of football's up-and-coming offensive minds thanks to his success as an assistant coach at the University of Michigan (1986 to 1993) under legendary Coach Bo Schembechler and as the quarterbacks coach for the NFL's Washington Redskins (1994 to 1996).

Worn for just one game in 1997, former Hoosier and current Temple University Athletic Director Pat Kraft's black jersey is encased on the second floor of long-time Bloomington bar Nick's.

Photo by John C. Decker.

Cameron's immediate goal when he returned to Bloomington was to change the conversation about Indiana football.

"We were coming off a couple of years where we had gone 1–15 in the Big Ten, and everything was so negative," says former IU football media relations director Todd Starowitz. "He wanted people talking about Indiana football in a different way."

That meant making changes, both subtle and dramatic.

One of the biggest changes came during fall camp. Instead of conducting all of August's fall training camp practices on the IU campus, Cameron chose to take his team on the road for a four-day barnstorming tour around the state. Those practices—which were only given approval by the NCAA once IU pledged not to promote the sessions—were held in Indianapolis, South Bend, Evansville, Fort Wayne, and Terre Haute, all with the goal of sparking fan interest in a program that had played host to an average of fifteen thousand empty seats at its home games in 1996.

Cameron also started laying the groundwork to do away with the artificial turf that had been the playing surface of choice in IU's Memorial Stadium since 1970. That change came about in 1998, when IU switched to natural grass.

But the change that is remembered most is the decision to design and ultimately wear black uniforms.

★ ★ ★

The black uniform was part of Cameron's larger vision for IU's game-day appearance. Indiana abandoned the crimson color that had been used during Mallory's tenure, instead opting for a more traditional red that was used by most of IU's other athletic teams. The football program also adopted a new logo, one that bore a strong resemblance to one used by the San Francisco 49ers.

That logo was the first step in changing IU's game day appearance.

IU Assistant Athletic Director for Team Purchasing and Licensing Marty Clark, who was the football team's equipment manager at the time, remembers teaming with former IU marketing director David Brown in the quest to find a new logo and uniform design for the football program.

"We had made several trips to (Indianapolis apparel company) Logo Athletic, who we had a contract with, and no one really liked what we had come up with," Clark says.

"Finally, I said, 'We have to come back with something. Cam will be upset that this has dragged on so long.'"

So Clark and Brown headed to Logo Athletic unannounced, adamant about returning to Bloomington with some ideas to present to Cameron.

"We didn't have a meeting, no appointment," Brown recalls. "We just drove up and asked to see the lead designer and told him what we wanted. We basically just sat there and looked over his shoulder the whole time. I'm sure he was ready to pull his hair out."

What materialized in an afternoon of trial and error was a dual oval with an italicized IU in the middle of it. They threw in some red, added a drop shadow, and the two IU administrators' mission for that day was fulfilled.

"I just wanted to have something to bring back," Clark says.

While they had something to show, Clark was convinced Cameron would hate it. But to his surprise the first-year coach loved it. With the logo in place, IU unveiled their new uniforms soon afterward, showing off the home red and the road white jerseys at the Big Ten Kickoff Luncheon in July 1997. There were no black uniforms at that event, but Cameron did hint to the assembled media that a third outfit could surface in the future.

"Cam wanted a secret uniform that no one knew about, one that would be used for special occasions," Brown says.

That special occasion came quickly.

* * *

After Indiana opened the season a month later with a respectable 23–6 loss at eighth-ranked North Carolina and a 33–6 win over Ball State, the Hoosiers prepared for a home match-up with rival Kentucky. The night before the game, Brown was at a pep rally and heard rumblings Cameron wanted to wear the black uniforms.

"I pulled Cam aside at the pep rally and asked him about the rumors, and he said the players were trying to convince him to do it, but he wasn't sure yet," Brown says. "He said, 'We'll see what happens tomorrow.'"

The decision, though, appeared to have already been made. Earlier in the day, Clark says he received a call from Cameron, who said he wanted to do something special for the Kentucky game and wanted to wear the black uniforms.

There were two issues with that plan: the jerseys weren't quite finished and they were in St. Louis.

With fewer than twenty-four hours before kickoff, Clark made the eight-hour round-trip drive and picked up the jerseys himself, returning to Bloomington late that evening. By the time the players arrived Saturday morning for the 2 p.m. kickoff, the jerseys were hung in each player's locker.

"The players had a great reaction to them," Clark says. "Black was a trendy color, something different, something unique."

Pat Kraft, a player on IU's 1997 team, said he had no idea they'd be wearing black jerseys until they entered the locker room. When he did see them, he was excited.

"It was a big deal—it was different and a pretty amazing switch from what was going on in college football at the time," Kraft said. "It was so cool."

In today's era of college football, alternate uniforms are commonplace. Most credit the University of Oregon and alumnus/Nike cofounder Phil Knight with this phenomenon. But it wasn't until the mid-2000s that Oregon began consistently changing the look of its uniforms throughout the season.

Other schools and uniform companies have followed suit, including Indiana. In 2013, Indiana unveiled six helmet designs, each of which has been worn at various times during the last five seasons. The Hoosiers also wore a new "candy stripe" football jersey for a 2016 match-up against Nebraska.

But in 1997, alternative jerseys were virtually nonexistent. Other than the Notre Dame green jersey—which dates back to legendary coach Knute Rockne and the 1920s—teams wore traditional home and away jerseys almost without exception. "Back then there was no Oregon, there was no Under Armour doing different things. It was kind of a cosmic shift in what college football was doing," Kraft said. "And then the game happened."

Kentucky came to Bloomington with their own first-year head coach, Hal Mumme. But unlike Indiana, which Clark said was "basically starting over as a program," the Wildcats had Tim Couch.

The Wildcats' sophomore quarterback arrived in Lexington after a decorated high school career in the Commonwealth State. After breaking national high school records for passing completions, yards, and touchdowns, he was tabbed as *USA Today*'s National Offensive Player of the Year in 1995 as a high school senior and later tabbed as ESPN.com's sixth-best high school athlete ever (as a high school basketball player he averaged 35 points per game as a junior and scored 3,023 career points).

After seeing limited playing time as a freshman under former Coach Bill Curry, Couch blossomed in Mumme's pass-oriented offense. He threw for a school-record 398 yards in UK's 1997 season-opening win against Louisville and then threw four touchdowns in a week 2 loss at Mississippi State. But his biggest fireworks were saved for Bloomington.

Couch threw for a Southeastern Conference record 7 touchdowns and 334 yards as Kentucky crushed the new-look Hoosiers, 49–7, the most lopsided victory in the series' history. While Couch was busy rewriting the UK, SEC, and Memorial Stadium record books, Brown had zero doubt about what he was witnessing from the Memorial Stadium sidelines.

"We went out there and got our asses kicked," Brown says. "We looked terrible."

At the game's conclusion, Hoosier players, coaches, and staff retreated to the Memorial Stadium locker room. Indiana's new look had done nothing to avoid the same old result for the long-suffering football program, and that September Saturday would prove to be the one and only time IU would wear the black uniforms.

But that's not where the story ends.

* * *

While Clark was disappointed in the game's result, he assumed there would be other games and better results for the black jerseys as Cameron went about building the IU program. That all changed, though, when one of Cameron's staff members—Special Assistant Dusty Rutledge—entered the locker room with a message.

"Dusty comes in probably thirty minutes after the game and said, 'You have to get these (black) uniforms laundered up now,'" Clark says. "My reaction was, 'What are you talking about?'"

Rutledge told Clark he'd talked to Cameron, who had just heard from Indiana basketball coach Bob Knight.

Knight—who had coached Cameron from 1981 to 1983 and was very much in support of his hiring—had shared his thoughts on IU's uniforms immediately after the game's conclusion. "(Knight) was upset," Clark says. "He told Cam we deserved to get our asses beat for wearing black because it's not our school color." But Knight didn't stop at sharing his opinion on the color of the uniforms. He didn't want to see those uniforms on the IU players again. And to ensure his request was honored, he demanded the uniforms be gathered and brought to his house.

Immediately.

"So I stayed, laundered them up, and boxed them up," Clark says. "And Dusty took them from me that night and took them to Coach Knight's garage."

Clark laughs at the fact that the highly anticipated jerseys were in St. Louis Friday night and were then banished from circulation twenty-four hours. But once they were in Knight's possession, no one in the know thought there was any chance they'd ever return.

"That was the end of the black experiment," Starowitz says.

"We never saw [the jerseys] again," Kraft says. "No one really brought them up, and as players you're curious, but at the same time, you're not. You're getting ready for the next game.

"But there was some talk in the locker room swirling around that someone wasn't very happy we wore them."

Rumors and whispers, though, were never enough to publicly produce the truth behind the reason for their disappearance. Cameron talked publicly about the fact Indiana wouldn't wear the black uniforms again but wasn't entirely forthcoming about the reasons for the decision.

If anything, Cameron's words sounded more like a public apology for concocting the idea in the first place.

"That wasn't real smart on my part," Cameron said at his weekly press conference three days after the UK defeat. "That's one thing I wouldn't do again. Indiana's colors are red and white and those are the colors you're going to see on Indiana football from now on.

"I looked out there and said, 'What the heck. That's not Indiana. What are we doing?'"

With those words, any thoughts of having the black uniforms reappear was put to rest publicly.

"They were gone forever—vanished," Kraft says.

But that's still not where the story ends.

The jerseys were gone, yes. But forever? No.

* * *

According to both Starowitz and Clark, the jerseys remained in Knight's garage for the next three years. Then came the fall of 2000, and Knight's dismissal as the Hoosiers' basketball coach.

Knight, the legendary and volatile IU basketball coach who led the Hoosiers to three national titles, had run afoul of former IU President Myles Brand. After a practice video surfaced in the spring of 2000 showing Knight putting his hands on a player's neck, Brand issued a nebulous "zero tolerance" policy for Knight's future behavior.

After a new allegation surfaced in the fall concerning an altercation between Knight and an IU student, Brand fired Knight, bringing an end to his twenty-nine-year run in Bloomington.

Six months later Knight was hired by Texas Tech to take over its basketball program, precipitating a move from his Bloomington home to Lubbock, Texas.

By this time, Cameron was in the midst of his fourth year (of his five-year tenure) with the Hoosiers, and the black jerseys had long been forgotten. But they resurfaced soon after Knight's dismissal, much to the surprise of Clark.

"They mysteriously showed back up here," Clark says. "One day, there were boxes of them, dropped off in the (basement) of Assembly Hall."

Indiana's all-time leader in total offense Antwaan Randle El was dressed in his number 11 jersey for the Hoosiers' 49–7 loss to Kentucky in 1997 but was academically ineligible to play that season.

Photo by David Brown.

Clark insists he doesn't know who brought them, or how they made their way back into IU's possession. He has his suspicions, but all are only best guesses, with the caveat he knows it wasn't Knight who returned them following his dismissal.

Brown, meanwhile, isn't necessarily sure how they got from Knight's house back to the IU Athletics Department either, but he does know how one of those forgotten jerseys ended up in his possession.

By 2000, Brown was no longer employed by the IU Athletics Department, having become the assistant athletic director for marketing at Ohio State in 1999. He returned to Bloomington the weekend of September 29, 2001, with the Ohio State administration for the IU-OSU football game and met up with then IU marketing director David Lovell, whom Brown had previously hired as his assistant.

"He says, 'Hey, I've got something for you,'" Brown says.

What Lovell had was an assortment of the black jerseys with the IU logo that Brown had helped bring to the program. Brown went through the box looking for one from an IU player of note. But that team was devoid of many superstars; the best known were defensive end Adewale Ogunleye (who spent eleven years in the NFL and was named to the 2004 Pro Bowl) and quarterback Jay Rodgers (who is now the defensive line coach for the Chicago Bears).

Brown ended up settling on a jersey of a player who didn't even dress for that game—Antwaan Randle El.

A freshman in 1997, Randle El sat out the season after being a partial academic qualifier out of high school. He made his way onto the field in 1998 and was Cameron's starting quarterback for the next four years. During those four seasons, Randle El

was one of the country's most dynamic players, earning 2001 Big Ten MVP honors. He currently ranks sixth in Big Ten history with 11,364 yards of total offense and second on IU's all-time lists in both rushing yards (3,895) and passing yards (7,469).

While Randle El is a prominent name in IU's record books, his unworn black uniform is almost as well hidden now in Brown's house as it was when it was tucked away in Knight's garage.

"That jersey is still hanging up in my closet as we speak," Brown says. "I'm not real sure why that jersey even exists since Antwaan couldn't play that year, but I've got it."

* * *

While Randle El's jersey hangs in Brown's closet, Kraft's jersey is the only one publicly displayed—at one of Bloomington's most popular bars, Nick's, of all places.

Unlike Randle El, who is recognized as one of the handful of greatest players in IU history, Kraft's Hoosier career included few headlines. He began his career as a walk-on before eventually earning a scholarship. His playing opportunities were sparse, with most of his contributions coming on special teams.

Obviously Kraft's jersey hasn't been on display for the better part of decade because of record-setting statistics but rather because of a good story shared over drinks.

In the mid-2000s, Kraft had returned to Bloomington to work on a master's in sports management (he would subsequently go on to earn his PhD from IU in sports management in 2008). One afternoon, he says, he was at Nick's while the bar was in the final stages of a second-floor renovation.

IU sports paraphernalia is littered throughout all levels of the ninety-year-old bar, and owners were deciding what new pieces to add. One that had already been hung was a football jersey worn by Yeronimo Ciriaco, a former Hoosier football player and staff member who had tragically died in an automobile accident in Champaign, Illinois, in 2004.

Kraft shared stories of Ciriaco—or "Mo" as he and his teammates called him. One of those stories was how Ciriaco and former IU football player and strength and conditioning coach Matt Bomba had mysteriously discovered and given Kraft his number 47 black jersey, which had also spent three-plus years in Knight's garage.

"The whole thing pretty much came about from a conversation over drinks," Kraft recalls. "They couldn't believe the story, and I said I'll go get mine and bring it in. I literally ran to my apartment because I didn't want them to change their mind about putting it up."

While Kraft did have to part with a very rare item, having it on display at his alma mater means plenty to him.

"Having it next to Mo's is special," says Kraft. "He's the reason I had it, and he was a special friend and person."

Now in his fourth year in charge of Temple's Athletics Department, Kraft's schedule doesn't provide many opportunities to get first-hand looks at his jersey. But he's still reminded about its presence on a regular basis.

"Hey—for me, getting my jersey up in a place like Nick's is a pretty huge achievement," jokes Kraft. "It's pretty cool. I still have people who send me photos of themselves by it."

Most of the other items that are hung at Nick's are collectibles from some of the greatest athletes, coaches and stories in the rich history of IU Athletics. There are items that commemorate NCAA Basketball Championships, bowl game victories, and Olympic gold medals.

Kraft's jersey, meanwhile, represents none of those. Instead, it's an artifact from a game that those involved couldn't forget about fast enough.

Why it remains, though, is because of an unforgettable—if not unbelievable—story.

"We didn't necessarily believe they were in Coach Knight's garage—it just seemed like a good Bloomington legend," Kraft says. "You hear the rumor, and it seems pretty outlandish. But eventually we find out—it was true."

Block? What Block?

John C. Decker

How many times have you seen former IU basketball player A. J. Moye's "play?"

Which one, you ask?

No, no one asks that question.

Everyone knows his "play" is the block of an attempted dunk by future NBA All-Star Carlos Boozer in the Hoosiers' Sweet 16 win over top-ranked Duke in 2002, a victory that helped propel IU to the national championship game.

It's a play that holds its own with Keith Smart's NCAA championship game winner in 1987, and Christian Watford's buzzer-beater against top-ranked Kentucky in 2011. Add in Kent Benson's last-second putback against Michigan in 1976 to force overtime and preserve IU's unbeaten season and Jay Edwards's top of the key 3-pointer to beat Michigan in 1989, and you have, arguably, the five most memorable IU basketball plays of the last forty years.

"I knew at the time, it was a pretty special play," Moye says fifteen years after the fact from his California home.

For those who do need a quick refresher, the 6'2" Moye didn't just block the 6'9" 280-pound Boozer's shot. He didn't just get a finger on it to ever-so-slightly steer it off course. He elevated up and over the much larger Duke center and denied both Boozer and the ball, never granting the ball permission to even exit the All-American's hands. When Boozer returned to the floor with the ball still in tow, the official's whistle blew, the ball was turned over to IU, and Moye had the defining play of his Hoosier career.

"People used to joke that I sent him to the second round [of the NBA draft] because 6'9" guys aren't supposed to get blocked by 6'2" guys," Moye says. But he did deny the dunk, and Moye's late second-half play—coupled with his 14 points—helped the Hoosiers overcome a 17 point deficit and upset the top-seeded Blue Devils, 74–73, in Lexington, Kentucky.

While it's been sixteen years since Moye helped orchestrate one of the biggest upset wins in school history, the play hasn't been forgotten. It's often featured during the IU men's basketball pregame highlight videos at Simon Skjodt Assembly Hall, and hundreds of thousands have subsequently watched it on YouTube—even though the video sharing website didn't exist until three years after the play originally happened.

So Hoosier fans have seen it—a lot.

But how many times have you seen the official box score from that NCAA East Regional semifinal game?

★ ★ ★

The box score is tucked away in a nondescript cardboard box in storage in Assembly Hall along with all of the other box scores, play-by-play accounts, and newspaper clippings from that season and many others. It offers the numeric details to the Hoosiers' one-point Sweet 16 win. Hoosier All-American Jared Jeffries had game highs of 24 points and 15 rebounds. Jarrad Odle added 15 points for IU. On the other side, Boozer led the Blue Devils with 19 points and 9 rebounds, while fellow All-Americans Mike Dunleavy (17 points) and Jason Williams (15 points) also scored in double figures for Coach Mike Krzyzewski's team.

And Moye?

The sophomore from Atlanta came off the bench to chip in 14 points, made 8 of 10 free throws (including a critical pair in the final seconds), had a pair of steals and . . . no blocks.

No blocks?

While Hoosier fans' memories, video highlights footage, and the NCAA statistician's manual insist otherwise, the written record of Indiana's improbable come-from-behind win will forever deny Moye credit for the play that he's remembered for most as an Indiana Hoosier.

That was news to Moye, who to this day can remember the most minute details of the play ("The ball got swung and dished down to Boozer, and Dane [Fife] was late rotating over,

Indiana 74, Duke 73

	1	2	Total
Indiana Hoosiers	29	45	74
(1) Duke Blue Devils	42	31	73

Indiana

	Pos	Min	FGM	FGA	3pM	3pA	FTM	FTA	Off	Def	Reb	A	Stl	BS	TO	PF	Pts
Jared Jeffries	F	38	9	21	1	3	5	7	9	6	15	1	2	1	5	2	24
Kyle Hornsby	F	16	1	4	0	1	0	0	0	2	2	2	0	0	2	1	2
Jarrad Odle	C	18	7	9	0	0	1	3	2	3	5	0	0	0	0	2	15
Tom Coverdale	G	29	1	3	0	1	4	6	1	3	4	7	1	0	2	4	6
Dane Fife	G	38	1	3	1	3	0	0	1	2	3	1	2	0	3	4	3
A.J. Moye		17	3	5	0	1	8	10	1	2	3	0	2	0	2	0	14
Jeff Newton		24	3	3	0	0	2	5	6	4	10	1	0	2	5	2	8
Donald Perry		17	1	4	0	1	0	0	0	4	4	1	1	0	4	1	2
George Leach		3	0	0	0	0	0	0	0	0	0	0	0	0	0	1	0
Team									0	1	1				0		
Total		200	26-52 (.500)		2-10 (.200)		20-31 (.645)		20	27	47	13	8	3	23	17	74

Duke

	Pos	Min	FGM	FGA	3pM	3pA	FTM	FTA	Off	Def	Reb	A	Stl	BS	TO	PF	Pts
Dahntay Jones	F	27	3	8	0	1	0	2	0	1	1	1	1	1	1	5	6
Mike Dunleavy Jr.	F	35	5	16	3	8	4	5	2	4	6	0	3	1	5	4	17
Carlos Boozer	C	35	7	10	0	0	5	9	8	1	9	3	2	1	3	3	19
Jason Williams	G	35	6	19	3	9	0	1	2	5	7	4	1	0	4	3	15
Chris Duhon	G	37	3	5	1	2	0	0	1	0	1	3	5	0	2	4	7
Casey Sanders		6	1	1	0	0	1	2	1	1	2	0	0	0	0	4	3
Daniel Ewing		25	2	8	2	4	0	0	2	1	3	1	2	0	3		6
Team									3	0	3				1		
Total		200	27-67 (.403)		9-24 (.375)		10-19 (.526)		19	13	32	12	14	3	16	26	73

Technicals - Ind 0. Duke 0.
Technicals (Coach/Bench) - Ind 0, Duke 0
Ejections - Ind 0. Duke 0.
Ejections (Coach) - Ind 0, Duke 0

Officials: David Hall, Bruce Benedict, Tony Greene
Attendance: 22,338
Arena: Rupp Arena
Location: Lexington, Kentucky, United States

The official box score from Indiana's win against top-seeded Duke in the 2002 NCAA Sweet 16 in Lexington, Kentucky, revealing that A. J. Moye wasn't credited with a block against Carlos Boozer late in the second half. Moye was instead credited with a steal and Boozer a turnover.

Courtesy of Indiana University Department of Athletics.

so I dropped down trying to make sure he couldn't lay it in"), but had never heard of its absence in the official account of the game.

"Honestly, until you brought that up, I had no idea I wasn't credited with a block," Moye says. "That's the first I've ever heard of it. I guess there must have been a Duke fan doing the stats."

Whatever the reason for the error, Moye says he's not surprised he was unaware of the omission. He insists he never looked at any box score after a game, a practice he adopted as a youth in Atlanta.

Moye said the practice came courtesy of Bill Russell, the legendary Boston Celtic center who won a pair of NCAA championships at the University of San Francisco (1955–56) before winning an NBA-best eleven world championship during a thirteen-year professional career in the NBA.

"I read Bill Russell's autobiography when I was about 12 or 13," Moye recalls. "Russell said one day when he was in college, he decided he'd stop checking the box scores and instead grade himself on just two things—winning and losing. From that day forward, he said that's when he started having success."

While Moye didn't approach Russell's unparalleled record of winning, he did win a pair of high school state championships at Westlake High School to go along with a Big Ten title and Final Four berth during his four years in Bloomington before embarking on a six-year professional career in Europe.

He's also the owner of one of the more memorable plays in IU basketball history—regardless of what the official box score says. "Honestly, when I was twenty years old, if I knew I wasn't credited with the block I'd probably have been pretty mad," Moye admits. "But since I've gotten older, with everything I've been through in life, it doesn't bother me at all."

That new perspective came in large part thanks to a life-changing health scare in 2010.

* * *

At the time, Moye was in his sixth year playing overseas. A standout with Deutsche Bank Skyliners in the German League, Moye collided with a Skyliner teammate in practice on November 15, 2010, and suffered a concussion. Moye said he thought he'd been knocked out for fifteen seconds due to the collision but subsequently found out it was fifteen minutes.

After returning to his Frankfurt home that evening, Moye said he knew something was amiss. He ultimately fell asleep and said he dreamed that he lost the mobility in his legs as well as the ability to talk and eat.

The following morning, Moye says the dream became his reality. "I woke up and I couldn't walk, I couldn't eat, I couldn't move the right side of my body," Moye says.

Despite his struggles, he still readied himself for that day's game against Maccabi Haifa, a team that included former Hoosier and teammate Marco Killingsworth. One of Moye's Skyliner teammates picked him up and drove him to the arena where he ultimately became disoriented on the court during warm-ups.

"I walked out on the court to try to shoot and I couldn't really see, couldn't walk," Moye says. "Marco came over and looked at me and said there was really something wrong."

Medical staff determined Moye suffered a stroke, and he was taken to a Frankfurt hospital. There, his condition worsened and he lay in a coma for two days. When he awoke, he says he didn't recognize family or friends who had come to be with him, including his seven-year-old daughter, Solana. "When I woke up, I really felt like I was in a fight for my life," Moye says.

His recovery was twofold. First, Moye says, doctors determined the stroke was caused by a congenital heart defect called a patent foramen ovale (PFO). A PFO is a small hole in the heart, and those who have it are at an exponentially higher risk for a stroke. Moye's condition was virtually identical to the one former NFL linebacker Tedy Bruschi had. Bruschi had a stroke in 2005 at thirty-one years old but ultimately returned to the field.

Moye's heart ailment required surgery, which was completed successfully in January 2011. But in the months prior to that procedure, he faced intense rehabilitation to attempt to regain as much mobility as possible.

"For two or three months, I really couldn't walk, couldn't talk, and really had to relearn everything," Moye says. "The doctors told me I might not be able to get back to where I was. They just didn't know."

While he was optimistic about his recovery, it wasn't until January 22 that Moye's confidence was affirmed. He said it was on that date that everything returned to normal. "For whatever reason, that was the day that I could suddenly walk, run, jump and remember things like before," Moye says. "Just one day, everything was back to normal."

Reflecting on those tough times, Moye says it was not only his faith that helped him persevere but also the outpouring of support from the Indiana basketball fans. While it had been nearly seven years since Hoosier fans had made the chant "Aaaa-Jaaaaay Moye! Aaaaa-Jaaaaaaay Moye!" a staple of Indiana home games, he was not forgotten now that he was thousands of miles away.

Word of his medical situation quickly circulated among Hoosier fans, many of whom reached out by email with well wishes and words of support.

"This is no lie—I received something like eighty thousand emails from IU fans," Moye says. "I was going through a dark time, and I'd spend an hour every day reading them. They helped build me back up. I was overwhelmed with them showing me that type of love. So to the people of Indiana, I say thank you. It's a special place. Even though I'd been gone for awhile, it was clear they loved me just the same as when I was there."

With the medical issues behind him, Moye faced a new challenge—deciding whether or not to continue his basketball career. At just twenty-nine years old, he was still young enough. His recent play, meanwhile, suggested he was still good enough as well. During the 2009–10 season, Moye averaged 18.6 points, 5.4 rebounds, and 1.7 assists playing for a professional team in Finland.

Fully cleared to train, Moye did just that in the months following his recovery. He believed there had been no drop-off in his game, and he had numerous inquiries about his interest in returning to play both in the US and overseas.

"When I came back and started to train, by July [2011], I felt I was ready to go," Moye says. "I felt like I was just killing it in workouts."

Despite getting the green light to play, Moye was aware that the concussion that precipitated the stroke wasn't his first. By his count it was his sixth, with two occurring when he was at IU and the others during his professional career.

"Suddenly a calm came over me, and I felt like a lot had been given to me, and it was time to give back," Moye says. "So I decided to retire from basketball."

The person he was most concerned about giving to was his daughter, Solana, who had stayed in Germany with him while he was recuperating. "Honestly, I think if I didn't have a daughter, I probably would have kept playing," Moye says. "But she made me realize there's more to life than basketball. She's the light of my life, the air in my lungs, and I want to give her a better life than mine. So when I thought about her, it was a no-brainer to stop playing."

★ ★ ★

With that decision made, the next challenge for Moye was deciding what to do next.

His first decision was to return to the US to see family. He headed to California, where he was reunited with his father, Malume, and his two younger brothers, Anson and Austen. Both had been toddlers when Moye first arrived in Bloomington as a college freshman in 2000, and A. J. had had limited involvement in their lives. By 2011, Moye's siblings were members of the Oaks Christian High School boys' basketball team just outside of Los Angeles, and they'd asked their older brother to help them train for the upcoming season.

What started out as an opportunity to build a stronger bond with his younger brothers quickly blossomed into much more. Moye began training both of his brothers, but soon, additional members of the Oaks Christian team joined in. Eventually, other area players asked Moye to work with them as well. The next thing Moye knew, he was asked to serve as an assistant coach at his brothers' high school for the 2011–12 season.

After one year as an assistant coach, Moye was named the school's head coach in 2012. He spent two years in charge of the program, helping develop future college players Chass Bryan (USC), Aleks Abrams (Cal Poly San Luis Obispo), Jordan Flannery (UC San Diego), and his brother Anson (Long Beach State). But after leading Oaks Christian to the Division IV-AA state championship game in 2014, Moye decided to leave to pursue other opportunities.

His departure from Oaks Christian didn't represent an exit from the game of basketball—far from it. His involvement in

After IU's upset of Duke, Moye and the Hoosiers upended Kent State and Oklahoma to earn a spot in the NCAA championship game. In IU's sixth-ever appearance in the NCAA championship game, Indiana fell to Maryland, 64–52, in Atlanta.

Photo courtesy of Indiana University Department of Athletics.

the sport is now twofold. He serves as assistant coach at Oak Park (CA) High School, which won the Class 3A state championship in 2016. He also serves as the master coach of basketball at the Sports Academy Foundation, where he trains some of California's elite youth basketball players as well as several professional players, among them, Nick Young (Golden State Warriors) and Jrue Holiday (New Orleans Pelicans).

When he moved to California he didn't necessarily see coaching and basketball training in his future, but he couldn't be happier with how things panned out. "I love my life," Moye says. "I knew (after I stopped playing) I wanted to be around the game that I loved. Basketball is part of my DNA."

He's also able to spend more time with his daughter. Moye said Solana will be living in California when she starts high school, and he's excited that basketball will no longer keep him from being involved in her life on a daily basis.

"She's exactly like me," Moye says. "She dresses like me, plays basketball like me. Now she's turning into a young woman.... She's my best friend. When I'm down and out, when I'm happy, when I'm sad, I can always share those experiences with her."

While Moye is excited about his new path in life, playing basketball is still something he can't completely get out of his system. He still plays with many of the players that he trains and says that they often encourage him to return to playing professionally.

But Moye says that isn't an option after his health scare.

"The thing about life is everyone at some point gets dealt an unfortunate hand. Sometimes it stinks. But you have to keep fighting and play the cards you're dealt," Moye says. "That's the story of my life—I've tried to take whatever circumstances I've faced on the court or in life and found a way to bounce back."

With his playing career behind him, Moye is fully committed to trying to create opportunities for today's youth basketball players. In some cases, it's training NBA-caliber players as they try to refine skills that are already among the world's best. In other cases, it's about trying to help a player develop to the point where they can earn a college scholarship, which in turn can open athletic and academic doors that wouldn't be available otherwise. And in some situations, it's about trying to help a player develop their skills to the point that they can make their high school basketball team.

No matter the goal, Moye has found it to be rewarding.

"I've been able to be a kid my whole life," Moye says. "I'm teaching the sport I love and I have the chance to spend time with kids and try to pass on some things that I've learned in my life. It's special."

It's also a special opportunity for those kids, who have an opportunity to learn the sport from a player who has won at the highest level in both high school and college, while also enjoying a successful professional career overseas.

Moye remains a bit of a cult figure among Hoosier basketball fans, but he admits that when he began training players in California, many didn't know who he was. Not only is he more than a decade removed from the conclusion of his college career, but he's also nearly two thousand miles from where he starred as a collegian.

But in this day and age, those California kids quickly found out who he was and why he's so well remembered by Indiana fans. "A lot of these kids weren't even in school yet when I was playing at Indiana, and having been overseas for a number of years, they really didn't know who I was," Moye says. "So I'd train them, and then they'd come back the next day and say they looked me up on YouTube and say, 'Hey, you blocked Boozer!'"

That he did—no matter what the box score says.

* * *

Like Hoosier fans, Moye won't soon forget that play, that game, or that 2002 season. Indiana captured the Big Ten title,

marking the program's first league crown since 1993. The improbable Final Four run was the school's first trip to the national semifinals since 1992, and the win over top-seeded

Duke is likely the program's biggest upset victory ever in the NCAA tournament.

"I love that team," Moye says. "That team was my favorite that I ever played on. I played on some great teams in high school, in AAU, teams that won titles as a pro. But that team, we were a band of brothers. We would do anything to help each other be successful."

Successful they were. Jared Jeffries was named the Big Ten's Most Valuable Player, and guard Dane Fife was tabbed as the league's Defensive Player of the Year. Tom Coverdale led the Big Ten in assists, and Jeff Newton led the conference in blocks.

Soon after recovering from a stroke suffered in 2010 while playing for the Deutsche Bank Skyliners team, Moye retired from the sport and turned his attention to coaching and training youth basketball players.

Photo courtesy of Indiana University Department of Athletics.

But for all of those individual accolades, what 2002 will be remembered for was the victory over Duke and Moye's defining play as an Indiana Hoosier.

"[The win over Duke] was a beautiful moment—exhilarating," Moye says. "Those final ten or fifteen minutes of that game, it was the most exciting basketball of my life.... As for the play—a lot of people remember that play, and that's humbling. It's human nature to want to be remembered for something. Eventually I hope I'm remembered for more than just blocking a shot.

"But maybe that was my moment in time."

3

Hep Creates Tradition That Rocks

Pete DiPrimio

Did a higher power help choose Hep's Rock?
It depends on belief, perspective, and a sunlight spotlight.

Hep's Rock looms just outside the Memorial Stadium weight room, just beyond the fireworks infrastructure in the north end zone that launches the Hoosiers into every game. It is a multiton gray chunk of limestone originally blasted out of the earth during the construction of Memorial Stadium back in the late 1950s. The name refers to Terry Hoeppner, the dynamic former Indiana football coach who passed before his time in the summer of 2007. Hoeppner is gone, but his memory lives on, both in the lives of the people he touched and in the rock that bears his nickname.

As players run onto the field before every game, they touch Hep's Rock as a sign of respect and a bid to tap into some of Hoeppner's motivational energy.

"When you walk out that tunnel and see Coach Hep's rock, it means a lot as far as what the man meant to the program," offensive lineman Coy Cronk said. "We've had people talk about Coach Hep and the passion he had for the game and the program... I wish I could have met the man."

Prentis Parker did meet the man. For years Parker was Indiana's facility caretaker. If there was a problem, he handled it. If something needed to be done, he took care of it. Parker quickly became a close Hoeppner friend, as just about everybody did. As we shall see, Parker had a pivotal role in finding and placing Hep's Rock.

"Coach Hep was one of the most fantastic ..." Parker stopped. His voice quivered. Perhaps that's the true measure of a good man, that he can touch people's hearts more than a decade after his death.

"I thought the world of him," Parker said. "The guy was awesome. If he would have lived, he would have had an awesome coaching run."

Brain cancer limited that run to two seasons, 2005 and 2006. Indiana went 4-7 in Hoeppner's first season and 5-7 in his second. It was enough to set the foundation for IU's 7-6 2007 season that included its first bowl appearance since 1993.

Along the way, Hoeppner prompted comparisons to Bill Mallory, the most successful football coach in IU history and as good a man as ever wore the Cream 'n' Crimson.

"Hep was like Coach Mallory," Parker said. "He was among the people I worked with that meant so much to me. He was the same way with the players that Coach Mallory was. They were both special."

Hep's Rock honors that.

"Having that rock there and knowing what he went through," Cronk said, "battling every day, just being a total warrior, it means a lot. You should take a lot of pride in that."

So the Hoosiers do, and woe to any player who treats it as a chair or a place to hang shoes, socks, or anything. The Rock isn't sacred, not in a religious sense, but it is meaningful.

"Sometimes you have young guys sitting on it, or players will put their shoes on it while we do walk-throughs," Cronk said. "We have to get on them about that."

For a while during the Kevin Wilson coaching era, Hep's Rock even had its own Twitter account in a whimsical attempt to capture Hoeppner's passion.

Where did Hep's Rock come from?

How did it come to rest in Memorial Stadium?

What was it about Hoeppner that was so inspirational?

Let's take a look.

Located behind the end zone on the north end of Memorial Stadium, the "Rock" is an Indiana Football tradition created by former coach Terry Hoeppner. Hoeppner coached the Hoosier program for two years before being diagnosed with brain cancer. He passed away in 2007.

Photo courtesy of Indiana University Department of Athletics.

* * *

Hoeppner arrived in December of 2004 from a successful run at Miami of Ohio. He was Hoosier born and bred, a native of Woodburn, a multisport standout at Woodlan High School, just outside of Fort Wayne in northeastern Indiana.

He was hired to restore the glory of Old IU, or at least that which existed during Mallory's bowl-making glory days of the late 1980s and early 1990s. The Hoosiers had stumbled into mediocrity under Cam Cameron and Gerry DiNardo. Hoeppner arrived with enough optimism for ten men. Some might have seen Indiana as a coaching wasteland (losing records were as common as a cold) or a stepping-stone job.

Renamed "Hep's Rock" in 2010, the limestone boulder was originally unearthed during Memorial Stadium's construction in the 1950s. Since its debut before the 2005 season, it's been tradition for all players and coaches to touch the rock as they enter the field before all Indiana home games.

Photo courtesy of Indiana University Athletics.

Hoeppner insisted it was his dream opportunity.

A few months after taking over the program, Hoeppner was looking for something to show that dream, something to inspire players and fans, something to represent his vision of what a football Hoosier really was.

Mark Deal was there. It seems like he's always been there in some form, either as a player or a coach or an administrator. "It was in May of that first year," Deal said. "Hep was driving to work. He was coming down Seventeenth Street, going down the hill past St. Paul's Catholic Center. When you go down the hill, it's the coolest thing ever. You look up and— bam!—there it is. Memorial Stadium. You see that as a coach and you go, God, I get to work here.

"Hep felt the same way. He saw that big limestone stadium and said, that looks like a big rock. He and his wife, Jane, had been to a John Mellencamp concert in Terre Haute. Mellencamp sang his song, R.O.C.K in the U.S.A. That song pumped Hep up. That got him going. That was the genesis of it, of the rock."

The next day, Hep met with Parker. "He said, 'I need a mascot.' That surprised me." Parker said. "Then he said, 'I need a rock. I need a big rock.'

"So that's what I got him."

Limestone is widespread throughout Monroe County. Construction projects often have to deal with it. That was certainly true when workers were building Memorial Stadium. A lot of the rocks, some the size of huge boulders, were dumped in the area that is now between the Mellencamp Pavilion and

the IU Tennis Center. In time, the trees grew to hide much of the debris.

But not from inquisitive eyes and optimistic hearts. Parker went into the woods to see what he could find.

"I went looking around over there by the tennis center. I went over all those rocks, and underneath this big blue spruce I see this rock. It was right where they put it all those years ago."

It looked like it fit Hoeppner's request, so Parker went to find Hoeppner to get confirmation.

"That morning I got him. I told him, let's go for a ride. I wanted to see if this was what he was looking for."

The two men hopped in a golf cart, unaware that Cream'n' Crimson history was about to be made.

"We went back under that big blue spruce," Parker said. "He saw it and, so help me this is the truth, the sun was coming up. The light went right in the two holes you see in the rock, shined right through them and hit the ground."

It looked, for all the world, as if the heavens were speaking. "When Hep saw that he pointed to it and said, 'That's my rock. I want that one.'"

"So that's what we got him."

It wasn't as easy as it sounds. The rock is massively heavy—an estimated three tons—and was lodged between other big rocks. A construction crew needed two backhoes to lift and move the rock. B. G. Hoadley Quarries supplied a limestone base for it to sit on. The rock was secured to the base by driving rods in the back of it "to hold it steady so it won't fall over and hurt somebody," Parker said.

The rock didn't have a name. Not then. It was, simply, the Rock.

The day the rock was installed, Hoeppner, Parker, and the others involved with the project gathered for a group photo.

"It meant a great deal that he got the rock that he wanted," Parker said. Parker added that Hoeppner later gave him a small replica of the rock. "Every time I see it, I get very sentimental," Parker said. "It means a lot. It brings back great memories."

In December of that year, a massive headache sent Hoeppner to the hospital for the first of two surgeries to try to remove a growing tumor. He wore a bracelet to reflect his determination to fight no matter what.

"He'd always wear that and he'd always tell me to never give up," Parker said. "Never give up. He gave me one and I wore it all the time. I never took it off until it broke, and then I put it on a shelf at home where I keep things from people I worked for who did things for me. Every time I'd see his wife, she'd raise her right hand that had the bracelet, and I'd raise mine."

No one was giving up.

* * *

Hoeppner's lasting legacy pushed beyond his northeastern Indiana roots. He was a football standout at Franklin College, good enough to get an invitation to training camp for the NFL's St. Louis Cardinals and Green Bay Packers. When that didn't work out, he briefly played in the long-gone World Football League with the Detroit Wheels and Charlotte Hornets.

Hoeppner then began his love affair with coaching. He spent most of the 1970s at the high school level—five as a head coach—before returning to Franklin College. He spent six years there as the defensive coordinator before moving to Miami of Ohio.

He was an assistant coach at Miami for thirteen seasons, the last three as the defensive coordinator (Miami was 32-11-1 with Hoeppner running the defense), before taking over as head coach. Hoeppner led Miami to bowl games in 2003 and 2004. He was a finalist for the Paul "Bear" Bryant national Coach of the Year award in 2003 after Miami went 13-1 and was ranked tenth in the final AP poll.

Hoeppner left a lasting impression with Miami quarterback Ben Roethlisberger, who went on to win a pair of Super Bowls with the NFL's Pittsburgh Steelers. "Coach Hoeppner has inspired me to be who I am today," Roethlisberger said in a statement after the coach's death. "He has been a second father, a teacher and a friend.... He believed in me and I owe everything to him for where I am in life. I hold the deepest love and respect for him, his wife Jane and their family. He has been a role model for so many young men. I aspire to be as honorable and touch as many lives as Coach Hep. I will miss him more than words can describe."

In the aftermath of Hoeppner's death, then Penn State coach Joe Paterno said in a statement: "I admired him as a person and a football coach. I wasn't around him a whole lot since we haven't played Indiana [while Hoeppner was at IU], but during the time I spent with him at Big Ten meetings, you could see that he was a very honest and courageous person."

Also, former Michigan coach Lloyd Carr said in another statement that, "Terry Hoeppner was the embodiment of the very best qualities that are admirable in a coach. He was a man of integrity and passion; he loved his players and he loved the game. He represented the highest ideals of intercollegiate athletics. His legacy will endure, but his presence will be greatly missed."

In eight seasons as a head coach, Hoeppner compiled a 57-39 record, but his contributions went way beyond numbers.

At Indiana, one of his favorite sayings (he had a ton of them) was "Play 13." Given that it was a twelve-game regular season, that meant play in a bowl game. IU finally did, six months after his death in December of 2007. It was the Hoosiers' first bowl since 1993.

Hoeppner had a favorite poem that reflected his philosophy:

Don't Quit

When things go wrong as they sometimes will,
When the road you're trudging seems all uphill,
When the funds are low and the debts are high
And you want to smile, but you have to sigh,
When care is pressing you down a bit,
Rest, if you must, but don't you quit.

Life is queer with its twists and turns,
As every one of us sometimes learns,
And many a failure turns about
When he might have won had he stuck it out;
Don't give up though the pace seems slow—
You may succeed with another blow.

Success is failure turned inside out—
The silver tint of the clouds of doubt,
And you never can tell how close you are.

It may be near when it seems so far.
So stick to the fight when you're hardest hit—
It's when things seem worst that you must not quit.

Author unknown

★ ★ ★

How inspiring was Hoeppner?

"Those kids would have run through fire for him," Parker said. "I traveled with him on the road, and I saw it. Those were great years. Hep and Mallory were the best."

Hoeppner might have been at his inspirational best during his second season. A three-game losing streak had ruined a 2-0 start. The Hoosiers had just been crushed at home by Wisconsin, 52–17.

Next up was a trip to Illinois.

"The night before the game, we stayed at a hotel there," Parker said. "The team was supposed to meet in a ballroom. Something happened and the hotel had them meet in the bar.... Well Hep walked into that bar. He looked at the players and said, 'They don't do us that way at Indiana. Get on the bus.'"

"Buddy, he meant business. We got to the stadium and those kids won that game. He knew how to talk to them."

In fact, IU won 34–32. The team followed that win by upsetting fifteenth-ranked Iowa, 31–28.

The Hoosiers got smashed by top-ranked Ohio State, then turned the tables and smashed Michigan State, 46–21. They were 5-4 and a win away from bowl eligibility.

The win never came. They finished 5-7 and were out of the postseason.

That bowl would happen the next season. By then, Hoeppner was gone, but not forgotten.

The Rock was there, you see.

"It represented so much," Deal said. "It was a gimmick at first that Hep had. But then, when he got cancer it became much more than that. It was a symbol of his struggle against cancer.... He was such a rock. He fought so unbelievably. The Rock was such a motivation to so many people."

Former IU coach Bill Lynch, who was on Hoeppner's staff and who took over after Hoeppner became too ill to coach, wanted to ensure everyone remembered Hoeppner's legacy. He went to IU athletic director Fred Glass and said, "We need to name this Hep's Rock." Glass agreed. The name was changed in an official ceremony in November of 2010.

"Players touch the Rock as they run out onto the field," Deal said. "It probably doesn't mean as much to these players as it did ten years ago. You try to tell them, but they don't know."

In fact, they do know.

"When you first come here," veteran safety Tony Fields said, "you don't know much about it, but as you get older, you start to learn more about it and all the things Coach Hep went through.... It basically means that every time you step on that field, you fight. You battle through it. We fight for sixty minutes just like he did. That's what we try to do."

Battles don't guarantee victory, but they give you a chance. Hep's Rock reflects that as well.

"Hopefully our team thinks of the hard-hat mentality that Coach Hep had," former IU safeties coach Noah Joseph said. "You always tap the rock, tap the rock. You have to be a physical, go-to-work football team. That's what our team takes from that."

Joseph never coached under Hoeppner, but he did work for him during some off-season camps while Hoeppner was at Miami of Ohio.

"When I was a young coach, Miami of Ohio always had a one-day senior camp. It would have around 380 kids, and I'd always work it. I was at Eastern Illinois at the time. I'll never forget one year we had it and there was a big storm. There was a lot of lightning and thunder, just terrible weather. Coach Hep didn't flinch. He got all the coaches together and said, 'Sudden change. We have to respond, so here's what we're going to do.' Then he bam-bam-bam rattled it off. He got it all organized in ten minutes. We were doing (shuttle drills) in the hallway of a dorm. "That left a big impression. Things won't always be perfect and go by how you script it. Situations come up and you have to respond to adversity. How do you choose to respond?"

Joseph saw a more emotional example of that a few years later. Hoeppner was at IU and going through chemo. Lynch had taken over as acting coach, but Hoeppner remained involved by watching practice and sending suggestions to the coaches.

"I remember Coach Hep put sticky notes on everybody's desk from what he saw at practice. He wanted to make sure they understood what they needed to get corrected. That also had a great impact on me. How much passion he had for the game and for the coaches he was working with. That's what I think of when I think of Coach Hep," Joseph said.

Hep's Rock ensures that passion and toughness will remain part of the program.

"Hep was such a rock." Deal said. "He fought so unbelievably hard.... Now the Rock represents much more than Terry dreamed. It is such a tribute to him and his fight against cancer. How brave he was. I mean, he had two brain surgeries and never blinked. He was an amazing guy. You can't help but honor him and his legacy."

Hep's Rock does that and more.

★ ★ ★

Here's an image of Hoeppner's intensity and motivational firepower.

It comes from a cold February day in 2005. Hoeppner was just a few months into the job. He was in his windowless office in the bowels of Memorial Stadium. The North End Zone facility, which features a huge office that overlooks the football field, was still years away.

The conversation briefly turned to his second year as the Miami head coach. His players wanted to impress him by saying they wanted to take their names off the backs of their jerseys. They play for Miami, they said, and not for themselves.

Other coaches have granted this request because it is team above individual. But Hoeppner was not most coaches. He became animated. He found his coaching edge. "You don't want your names on the jersey?!" he shouted. "I'm not letting you take them off. I'm making you accountable." The more he talked, the more passionate he became. "You don't want to be accountable? You don't want to take personal responsibility? That TICKS me off!"

Hoeppner kept hammering that theme. "I want guys who are accountable and responsible. Then you can't hide. Who's number 6? Oh, I see. The name is right there for [the] whole world to see."

And then he delivered the kicker: "You play for the name on the front. You're accountable for the name on the back."

Hoeppner was accountable for the name on the back of the jersey.

In a lot of ways, he still is.

What's the Deal with IU Football?
Mark Knows

Doug Wilson

Every Hoosier fan knows about the Old Oaken Bucket.

Every serious Hoosier football fan also knows about Coach Bo McMillin's 1945 undefeated Big Ten championship football team, the only team in Indiana University history to avoid a setback in a season.

But there's more to be told about both than what's on the surface.

For instance, how many know about a more than seventy-year-old version of the Old Oaken Bucket trophy that's barely the size of a spool of thread?

Or how many can recount the tale about the photo of ten members of the 1945 team that once hung at a well-known establishment near campus, a place where one of the team's best players wasn't allowed to dine?

There's also the story about where the Old Oaken Bucket came from, and how it made a return trip to its original home— more than ninety years later.

No one knows these stories and many others about Indiana football better than Mark Deal, IU's assistant athletic director for alumni relations. Mark's father, Russ, was the captain of the 1945 Hoosier football team, and Mark grew up hearing stories about his father's team and the players that made it one of the nation's best. More than seventy years later, it's difficult to find anyone who knows the 1945 team as well.

As for the Old Oaken Bucket, it's Deal who keeps it under lock and key at Memorial Stadium when it resides in Bloomington. And when it instead spends a year calling West Lafayette home, there isn't anyone who craves its return more than Mark, a former Hoosier player, coach, and now administrator, whose passion for the program is unsurpassed.

That's why a tiny replica of the Old Oaken Bucket from 1945 means so much to him.

First, a little background on "the Bucket." According to written accounts from the Indiana University Archives, the real Old

Oaken Bucket came about nearly a century ago in a fashion that university employees today can surely still relate to: it was the product of a committee. In this case, it was a committee of Indiana and Purdue alumni who sought to establish a trophy of some sort for the two schools' annual rivalry football game.

IU President William Lowe Bryan reported the decision of the committee, after multiple meetings, in a Western Union telegram to IU athletics director Zora Clevenger on October 23, 1925: "Chicago Alumnae of Purdue and Indiana in a joint session last night decided to donate and establish as a playing trophy an Old Oaken Bucket with I or P links added yearly."

* * *

The Old Oaken bucket was established during the season of 1925. The inaugural Bucket game that year ended in a 0–0 tie, thus the trophy's handle is adorned with a block copper link that represents both schools.

Twenty years later, in 1945, players from both teams received a tiny replica of the Old Oaken Bucket to commemorate the Bucket's twentieth anniversary. Made of wood, it bears a paper logo with the same words as on the real Old Oaken Bucket—"Old Oaken Bucket, Purdue vs. Indiana, Established 1925." It's adorned with a tassel that was once cream and crimson, but has long since lost its color.

Not many of those tiny replicas exist today, at least according to Deal, who proudly owns one of them, handed down to him from his father, Russ. It can now be found encased in the Henke Hall of Champions, along with many other irreplaceable pieces of IU Athletics history.

It's an item that is on loan to IU Athletics from Deal, who cherishes the miniscule bucket as much as just about anything he's ever accumulated from a life around Hoosier football.

Mark's affinity for the Hoosiers can easily be traced back to his father, an All-American offensive tackle and captain of the

While most Hoosier fans know about the Old Oaken Bucket, very few are aware of the miniature Old Oaken Bucket that was given to Indiana captain Russ Deal in 1945, commemorating the twentieth anniversary of the first Old Oaken Bucket game between Indiana and Purdue.

Photo by John C. Decker.

1945 team. Russ later became known as the father of Hobart football after coaching at Hobart High School in northwest Indiana from 1948 to 1966, and he was elected to the Indiana Football Hall of Fame in 1976.

In 2013, eleven years after the death of their father, Mark and his brother Mike were also elected, the only father-son-son set of Indiana Football Hall of Famers. Mike played for Russ at Hobart High School and was an All-State halfback in 1964, while Mark also starred at Hobart High School and earned All-State recognition in 1974. "This is the biggest [honor] I've received as a professional, as a player or coach," Mark told the *Times of Northwest Indiana* at the time. "To be in a hall of fame that includes my father and now my brother is very, very special."

There aren't many families with closer ties to Indiana University football than the Deals. Russ Deal was an All–Big Ten and All-American at IU who also played in the Blue-Gray Football Classic All-Star game and the Chicago Charities College All-Star game. He was elected to the Indiana University Athletics Hall of Fame in 1993.

Mike Deal played on the 1967 Big Ten Championship and Rose Bowl team, and in the Blue-Gray All-Star game as well as the 1970 Senior Bowl.

Even in one of the ultimate IU sports families, nobody has been connected to Indiana football and the university like Mark Deal has. After earning All-State honors at Hobart High, he played center for Lee Corso's Hoosiers from 1975 to 1978 and began his coaching career as an IU graduate assistant in 1979. The 1979 squad finished with an 8-4 record, including a thrilling Holiday Bowl win (38–37) over Brigham Young University.

In addition to stints as an assistant coach at Wabash, Virginia Military Institute, Kansas State, Marshall, and Rutgers, he was IU's offensive line coach from 1996 to 1999 and has worked in IU Athletics administration since 2000.

Deal's wife, Patricia, is also an IU graduate. Their daughter, Carrie, played volleyball at IU in 2005 and 2006, earning

Academic All–Big Ten honors in 2006 and graduating with a degree in special education in 2009. Carrie is married to former IU quarterback Blake Powers.

The Deals are one of only two families in Indiana athletics history to have three generations of letter winners—and they are about to become the only family with four generations of letter winners. Riley Hecklinski, the granddaughter of Mark's brother, Mike, enrolled at IU in the fall of 2017 and plays softball for the Hoosiers. In addition, Mark and Patty's son, Casey, graduated from the Kelley School of Business in 2013.

And as for the Bucket—the Deal family leads the world in Bucket wins with 14.

This family history and a life lived in Cream and Crimson makes many things about Indiana athletics special to Mark, including a tiny wooden replica of the Old Oaken Bucket from 1945.

"I think it's probably pretty valuable, but I'd never sell it for anything," Deal said. "I'm not a collector of stuff. I'm a collector of stuff that means something to me."

★ ★ ★

Deal might not be willing to ever part with his replica bucket from 1945, but it is his responsibility to hand off the real traveling trophy when the game results of the regular season finale against Purdue dictates he do so.

So if you've ever wondered who it is that shoulders that burden, it's the person who probably cringes at the thought of seeing it depart from Indiana's halls more than anyone else. Fortunately for Deal, recent series success has kept it in IU's possession more often than not. The four straight wins against Purdue from 2013 to 2016 equaled the Hoosiers' longest winning streak in the rivalry, matching the four straight games won from 1944 to 1947.

But all good things come to an end at some point, and Deal takes his responsibility of handing off the trophy seriously. He said that when Purdue loses, an equipment manager usually

sets the Bucket on the field and leaves it for IU to retrieve. By contrast, Deal feels it is important to show class when the time comes to give the Bucket back to the Boilers, even though it is painful. "I always take it to a player, shake their hand, and congratulate them."

Deal recalled the time in 1976 when Purdue, winner of four straight Bucket games, was so confident about winning that the Boilermakers didn't even bring the trophy with them to the game, so it had to be retrieved after a 20–14 Indiana win, the first of two straight for Corso's Hoosiers against Purdue.

The Old Oaken Bucket is considered one of college football's best rivalry trophies, alongside the likes of the Floyd of Rosedale (Iowa vs. Minnesota), Paul Bunyan's Axe (Wisconsin vs. Minnesota), and the Victory Bell (UCLA vs. USC).

Photo courtesy of Indiana University Athletics.

Given Deal's family history, the responsibility to be Indiana's keeper of the Bucket is special. "I get emotional," he said. "It's been a crusade for my family for all our lives, even when we were kids and would go with our dad to the Old Oaken Bucket game."

* * *

While Deal doesn't relish the thought of handing off the Old Oaken Bucket to a Purdue player after a Boilermaker win, there was a recent time that he presented the Bucket to someone else that created a cherished memory.

In 2016, IU Athletics received a phone call from a descendant of the Bruner family, the family that donated the Bucket to the school in 1925. That phone call came from Lisa Bruner, who wanted to talk to someone about the exact origin of the Old Oaken Bucket at a farm in southeastern Indiana.

Who else could the department assign to handle such a call other than Mark Deal?

That farm, between Kent and Hanover, was owned by William and Cora Bruner, who donated the Bucket in 1925. One colorful version of the story of the farm and the bucket says that Confederate general John Morgan once drank from it during his incursion into Indiana in the midst of the Civil War in the summer of 1863. There's been no confirmation about the General Morgan part of story, but Deal did help the Bruners celebrate their successful research project. The family was able to find the site of the Bruner farmhouse, whose exact location had been lost after the family had sold the farm decades ago.

Deal made two trips to the old Bruner farm. On the second visit, he brought the Bucket with him and was welcomed by Lisa and her husband, Bill Bruner. Bill is the great-grandson of William and Cora Bruner, who lived in the farmhouse long before the Old Oaken Bucket existed and before a well in front of the farmhouse had been covered.

"I went there for the first time and saw the well where the Bucket came from. I got chills," Deal said. "When I went back the second time, it was the first time the Bucket had been there since October 1925."

According to Deal, it was Bill's Aunt Bonnie who eventually tracked down the location of the farmhouse by helping Bill and Lisa retrace the route from memory. But they never would have gone looking in the first place if it wasn't for a letter. Bill's dad, Clayton, had written a letter to IU Athletics years ago, hoping that because of his family's connection to the Bucket, he could attend a game and present the Old Oaken Bucket to the winner. He never mailed the letter, which was written in 2003. But in 2015, while Clayton was living in a nursing home in Cincinnati, a member of the family discovered the letter. As a result, Lisa started looking for more information in hopes of honoring her father-in-law's wishes.

Lisa learned of the Bruner family farmhouse during her research, but didn't initially find its exact location. After she contacted Deal, he arranged to have the Bucket brought to a hospital where Clayton was staying, but Clayton died before that could happen. Lisa, working with Aunt Bonnie, eventually found the site of the Bruner farm and made arrangements with Deal for the Bucket's return home.

Standing on the well, Deal presented the trophy to the Bruners in an official ceremony, reciting the lines of the Samuel Woodworth poem "The Old Oaken Bucket," which inspired the trophy's inception.

How dear to this heart are the scenes of my childhood,
When fond recollection presents them to view!
The orchard, the meadow, the deep-tangled wildwood,
And every loved spot which my infancy knew;
The wide-spreading pond and the mill which stood by it,
The bridge, and the rock where the cataract fell;
The cot of my father, the dairy-house nigh it,
And e'en the rude bucket which hung in the well,—
The old oaken bucket, the iron-bound bucket,
The moss-covered bucket which hung in the well.

That moss-covered vessel I hail as a treasure;
For often, at noon, when returned from the field,
I found it the source of an exquisite pleasure,
The purest and sweetest that nature can yield.
How ardent I seized it, with hands that were glowing!
And quick to the white-pebbled bottom it fell;
Then soon, with the emblem of truth overflowing,
And dripping with coolness, it rose from the well;—
The old oaken bucket, the iron-bound bucket,
The moss-covered bucket, arose from the well.

How sweet from the green mossy brim to receive it,
As, poised on the curb, it inclined to my lips!
Not a full blushing goblet could tempt me to leave it,
Though filled with the nectar that Jupiter sips.
And now, far removed from the loved situation,
The tear of regret will intrusively swell,
As fancy reverts to my father's plantation,

And sighs for the bucket which hangs in the well;
The old oaken bucket, the iron-bound bucket,
The moss-covered bucket which hangs in the well.

★ ★ ★

There's no argument about which was the greatest football team in the history of Indiana football.

That honor goes to the 1945 squad, captained by Mark's father, Russ. Featuring some of the program's all-time greats such as George Taliaferro, Pete Pihos, and Howard Brown, Coach Bo McMillin's team went 9-0-1 overall and 5-0-1 in the Big Ten. It remains the only undefeated team in school history.

Despite playing all but one of its six Big Ten games on the road, the team outscored its league opponents 279–56. Only a 7–7 tie with Northwestern in the second game of the season stood in the way of perfection.

Four of Indiana's nine wins came via shutout, including three straight to end the season—49–0 over Minnesota, 19–0 against Pitt, and a 26–0 blanking of Purdue.

"That '45 team was as good as they get; it's the greatest in our history," says Deal. "It's a different era, but they never lost. They were talented and they were deep. Defensively was where they really shined. That was probably the best defense ever."

Indiana finished No. 4 in the final '45 national rankings, behind only Army, Navy, and Alabama.

There are a number of historical pieces from the '45 team, ranging from game programs to game tickets. But one of the most interesting items is a photo that hangs in the Henke Hall of Champions. This photo of ten starters from the squad previously resided in the Gables restaurant in downtown Bloomington shortly after the magical 1945 season. The full-color picture is approximately twelve feet wide and four feet high and still bears splatter stains from the Gables soda fountain.

The Gables, which was open from 1931 to 1980, was located in a historic building on South Indiana Avenue, across from where the Maurer School of Law can be found today. It's now home to BuffaLouie's restaurant. Before becoming the Gables, the building housed the Book Nook, where Bloomington's legendary jazz composer and songwriter Hoagy Carmichael wrote part of his American classic, "Star Dust," in 1927.

The photo of the 1945 team features right end Ted Kluszewski, right tackle John Goldsberry, right halfback Dick Deranek, right guard Howard Brown, fullback Pete Pihos, center John Cannady, left halfback George Taliaferro, left guard Joe Sowinski, quarterback Ben Raimondi, left tackle Russ Deal, and end Bob Ravensberg. In the era of two-way football, many of those players were the team's defensive stars as well.

The photo was, and still is, an eye-catching tribute to the only undefeated season in the history of IU football, one of only two teams in the program's history to win the conference title.

The most famous of those players for what he accomplished on and off the field at IU and in his life after college was Taliaferro, a Merrillville, Indiana, product who was a freshman in 1945.

One of the program's all-time greats, Taliaferro would go on to be the first African-American drafted in the NFL, selected by the Chicago Bears in the thirteenth round in 1949. Instead of beginning his pro career in the NFL, though, he instead played with the Los Angeles Dons in the All-American Football Conference and was named the league's Rookie of the Year.

Taliaferro jumped to the NFL the following year, signing with the New York Yanks. His six-year NFL career included stints with the Yanks (1950–51), Dallas Texans (1952), Baltimore Colts (1953–54) and Philadelphia Eagles (1955). The second African-American to ever play quarterback in the NFL, Taliaferro earned Pro Bowl honors in 1951,

1952 and 1953. Among many awards, Taliaferro was inducted into the College Hall of Fame in 1981, awarded the National Football Foundation and College Hall of Fame Distinguished American Award in 2011, and received Indiana's Sagamore of the Wabash award in 2012.

While that photo represents a nod to him and his teammates from the '45 squad, it also includes some regrettable history about Bloomington and Indiana University.

During the 1940s, the university and the city of Bloomington were segregated. Among many other things, that kept Taliaferro from being admitted to the restaurant where the picture hung, the Gables. When Indiana University President Herman B Wells found out that Taliaferro was forced to run home between classes to eat lunch because no nearby restaurant would serve him, Wells phoned the Gables and told the manager that he and Taliaferro would be eating there that day. When the manager balked at the idea, Wells suggested if that was the case, then he'd make the Gables off limits to the entire student body.

The manager relented, Taliaferro and Wells ate at the Gables, and a big step was taken toward desegregating local eateries.

* * *

Two of the key players on that 1945 team weren't around when the season started, but they made a huge impact once they returned ... from the war.

The previous year, Indiana had finished with a 7-3 record and placed fifth in what was then the Big Nine Conference. The 1945 season began shortly after World War II ended, and the Hoosier roster got a significant boost with the return of several players from military service.

After spending years above the soda fountain at the Gables restaurant in Bloomington, this iconic photo of eleven members of the Hoosiers' 1945 football team was turned over to IU Athletics, which displays it in the Henke Hall of Champions.

Photo by John C. Decker.

Nine players who had previous playing experience rejoined the team just as the season began after serving in the United States Armed Forces. Headlining that group was Pihos and Brown.

During his military service, Pihos served in the Thirty-Fifth Infantry under George Patton and was part of the group that on June 6, 1944, stormed the beaches of Normandy on D-Day. Ultimately, Pihos received a battlefield promotion in the Battle of the Bulge from Patton and was awarded the bronze and silver medals for bravery.

Upon his return to Bloomington in 1945, he made an immediate impact for Coach Bo McMillin's squad as the team's fullback.

"My dad and George Taliaferro both said Pete Pihos was the best football player Indiana has ever had," said Deal. "And they both watched [1989 Heisman Trophy runner-up] Anthony

Players with Old Oaken Bucket, (*left to right*) Alvin Nugent "Bo" McMillin, Pete Pihos, Russell Deal, Melvin H. Groomes, George Taliaferro, 1945.

Thompson and [2001 Big Ten Most Valuable Player] Antwaan Randle El play."

Pihos joined the likes of Taliaferro and eventual College Football Hall of Fame quarterback Ben Raimondi to give McMillin a plethora of playmakers in the backfield.

"There's probably never been a backfield like that in IU history with two All-Americans," Deal said.

Brown was equally decorated for his military service during World War II, and equally important to the team's success upon his return. Like Pihos, he was granted a leave from the military so that he could return to Bloomington and play football while he waited for his official discharge.

The recipient of three Purple Heart citations for his service, Brown also returned after the Hoosiers' season-opening win and immediately anchored the team's offensive line as the team's right guard.

"Bo McMillin said they won because the [offensive] line was so good," Deal said. "Howard Brown was actually the team MVP with all of those stars they had. The dominance of the offensive line was never more evident than in the shutout of twentieth-ranked Purdue, when the Hoosiers piled up 349 yards on the ground while dominating their in-state rival in the regular-season ending contest.

At that point, the Big Nine Conference had no bowl affiliation—in 1946, it would begin its relationship with the Rose Bowl. So, the Hoosiers' season ended with the 26–0 win over Purdue.

There were talks that the nation's top-ranked team, Army, and fourth-ranked Indiana would play in a bowl game at Soldier Field in Chicago, Deal said, but that never came to

fruition. Instead, Indiana finished the greatest season in program history two days after Thanksgiving.

"Indiana vs. Army would have been special," Deal said. "But it wasn't meant to be. Army and Navy, which finished ranked number 2, were both tremendous and talented. They could recruit players from other teams during the war and Army even had one of Indiana's former stars on its team. But that Indiana team wouldn't have backed down against Army. I guarantee it."

After the season, honors rolled in for the Hoosier players.

Pihos finished eighth in the voting for the 1945 Heisman Trophy after rushing for 410 yards and seven touchdowns. He received first- or second-team All-American honors from a slew of outlets, including the UPI, Associated Press, and *The Sporting News*. He was also tabbed as a first-team All-Big Ten choice by both the AP and UPI, and he would later be inducted into both the College Football Hall of Fame and the Pro Football Hall of Fame.

Taliaferro shared the backfield with Pihos and led the Big Nine Conference with 719 rushing yards on 156 carries as a freshman. Like Pihos, he was named to a large number of All-America squads, including a second-team nod from *The Sporting News*. He earned first-team All-Big Ten honors from both the AP and UPI, and he would also eventually be inducted into the College Football Hall of Fame.

Others were also honored. End Bob Ravensberg was probably the most decorated player following the season, a consensus first-team All-American who was put on the first-team squad by three different outlets. Fellow end Ted Kluszewski—who would go on to play major league baseball for fifteen years—was a first-team All–Big Ten choice by both the AP and UPI. Tackle John Goldsberry, meanwhile, received second-team All–Big Ten from the UPI.

All of those eventual postseason award winners are featured on the 1945 picture that is among the centerpieces of the Henke Hall of Champions.

Oddly enough, it is actually one of two oversized pictures of the 1945 team that can be found around town. In addition to the one that is in IU Athletics' possession, there's another photo at the Alley Bar, a local watering hole located just west of the downtown square. While some confuse that photo with the one that was originally located at the Gables, Deal says the one at the Alley Bar was actually taken before the Hoosiers' November 17 game against Pitt that year. Several of the team's more prominent players—including Taliaferro—aren't included in that photo, as some of the players had yet to arrive in town for the Pitt contest when it was taken.

Nonetheless, both photos do their part to remind Hoosier fans about the greatest team in the history of the program. It's a team that had to go on the road to play all of its Big Ten games except the Purdue game because other Big Ten foes didn't respect the IU program enough to agree to travel to Bloomington to play, according to Deal.

That didn't stop the team from dominating its foes like no other Indiana team ever had or has since.

"The greatest in our history," Deal said.

5

Hoosier History Com-Pyled

John C. Decker

Yellowed pages with frayed edges tell some of the most compelling stories of Indiana University Athletics from days long since passed.

From 1922 until the early 1960s, the historical record of all IU's athletic teams were compiled by Indiana University students. Annually, undergraduates would apply to serve as "managers" for IU's various sports. Those who were ultimately selected to fill those roles were entrusted with a long list of duties and responsibilities for their respective sport, including team travel, team finances, visitor accommodations, and marketing, among others.

"At that point in time, you're talking about an athletic administration that was very small," says IU Assistant Athletic Director Chuck Crabb, a forty-seven-year veteran of IU Athletics. "Probably an athletic director and a business manager and that's it. The managers served a critical role for every team."

One of the many responsibilities of these student managers was to compile the "manager's book" for their sport as an official record of the details and performances of players and seasons past for future generations. The end result was a bound edition for each sport, complete with many things you'd expect to find—and others that you wouldn't.

Game results, programs, player statistics, newspaper clippings, and photographs are accompanied by train tickets, dinner receipts, telegraphs, and other miscellaneous items that managers felt relevant to include to tell the tale of that particular season. All reveal a bygone era of intercollegiate athletics and, in many cases, society.

Kit Klingelhoffer, a former IU media relations director who spent forty-two years in the IU Athletics before retiring in 2012, is well aware of the books' contents as well as their significance. "There's a lot more in there than just the box scores—it's really the behind-the-scenes stuff that is fascinating," Klingelhoffer says. "Someone owes a big clap of the hands to those managers

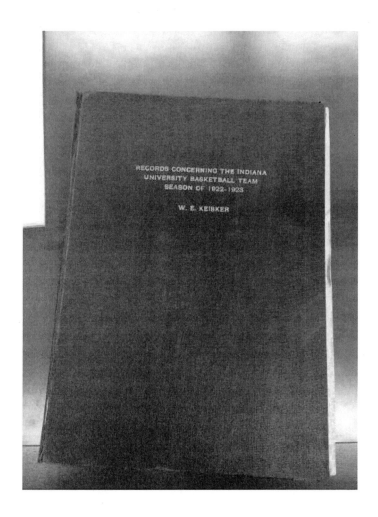

who kept those books through the years. They were devoted and deserve a lot of credit. To use an old [former IU football coach] Bill Mallory term, 'They didn't slop around.'"

While these books share the details of countless road trips made by IU's varsity teams, they themselves have an interesting tale of where they've been in their own right. While they're now preserved in a controlled environment at the IU Archives in Wells Library, their nearly one-hundred-year journey has often put them in less-than-ideal situations for their preservation.

Crabb said when he started working in IU Athletics in 1970 as an undergraduate student assistant in the Sports Information Department (now called Media Relations), the books were kept in an office library, which at the time was in a Quonset hut located where present day Cook Hall can be found.

Once the publicity offices were moved inside of Assembly Hall, the manager's books came along as well. They subsequently bounced around from closet to cubicle over a thirty-plus year period, always close enough to be called on for reference needs, but rarely in a location that took their long-term well-being into account.

Dating back nearly one hundred years, the IU athletics manager's books have bounced around between various buildings, storage cabinets, and closets before finally being moved to the IU Archives in Wells Library to preserve them for future generations.

Photo courtesy of Indiana University Archives.

"We've had these books in air-conditioned spaces with no humidity control, we've had them in boxes in closets that had no HVAC of any variety," Crabb says. "For the longest time, they were in areas of Assembly Hall that had been intended to be elevator shafts and were converted into storage. Those aren't the best conditions for records that fragile."

Considering their age and less-than-optimal maintenance, the books remain in relatively good shape. In some instances the books' bindings have begun to give way, and in others, the glue holding photographs in place has long since failed. But they still reveal many interesting tales of Indiana Athletics, beginning with their first book—the 1922 edition for football.

* * *

That book was compiled by the sport's first senior manager who was well known on campus, and would eventually become well known around the world—Ernie Pyle.

Pyle is best known as the Pulitzer-Prize-winning journalist whose syndicated newspaper column detailed the lives of everyday Americans in the 1930s and 1940s. His early columns focused on those in rural America, before he turned his attention to US soldiers when he was an embedded journalist during World War II. He was eventually killed by enemy fire near Okinawa, Japan, in 1945.

But long before his column was being picked up by more than three hundred newspapers, he was an IU undergraduate student making significant contributions on the Bloomington campus. He wrote for the school's yearbook, the *Arbutus*, as well as the student newspaper, the *Indiana Daily Student* (*IDS*). He would eventually serve as the *IDS*'s editor in the summer of 1922.

Upon completion of his stint as newspaper editor, he turned his attention to athletics.

In the fall of 1922, Indiana University debuted its "Student Manager Plan," which was unveiled after reviewing what other schools within the Western Conference (now called the Big Ten) and other East Coast universities were doing to enhance their athletics programs. The plan placed particular emphasis on the sport of football, which would have one senior manager, two junior managers, and four sophomore assistants.

Pyle was tabbed as the first senior student football manager—and thus the first student manager in any sport. In addition to his knowledge of athletics and his leadership experience from his time with the *IDS*, another reason Pyle was selected for the position, according to the September 16, 1922, edition of the *IDS*, was the resourcefulness he showed "by bumming 28,000 miles across the Pacific and back on only $200 and bringing a Filipino student back from Manila to enroll in Indiana University."

The 1922 Indiana football manager's book, unfortunately, isn't filled with the poetic words of Pyle. Instead, it was compiled by one of two junior managers, Vern Ruble. But through the included newspaper reports, it shows Pyle to be a creative and outlandish marketer for a team that was shut out five times in seven games and ultimately finished 1-4-2 under first-year coach Pat Herron.

In the final weeks of the season, Pyle helped oversee fundraising efforts to allow the one-hundred-member IU band to travel to the November 25 season-ending game against Purdue. The November 18, 1922, edition of the *IDS* details an "auto polo" match as well as a "mule polo" contest at the then home field of the IU football team, Jordan Field.

Located where the Indiana Memorial Union parking lot can be found today, these contests were bizarre; the auto polo match featured Pyle driving in one car and fellow IU student Barrett Woodsmall driving the other. Each driver had a second passenger—or "mechanician"—who wielded a croquet mallet and attempted to bat a basketball into the goal on either end of the field. The cars, meanwhile, had the outer bodies removed, leaving the passengers exposed. To provide some degree of protection, each was fitted with "hoops" over the top in case either rolled over.

Additional precautions were also taken. The November 16 edition of the *IDS* said, "Pit crews and hospital corps for each car have been organized in case of casualties either to the cars or the occupants." All passengers ultimately escaped unharmed.

The game of mule polo, meanwhile, was even more odd. According to the *IDS* account, Ruble rode one of the animals, while Art Coulter rode the other. Armed with brooms, each paraded around the field and attempted to knock a basketball into the goal. The goal, meanwhile, was defended by fellow student Merritt Read, who was on top of a horse.

Those matches were accompanied by another out-of-the-norm competition during the three-hour-plus fundraising event. Pyle and event organizers also held a "Fat Man's Marathon Championship" race around the Jordan Field track.

Open only to Indiana University students who weighed at least 240 pounds, entrants raced four hundred yards in an effort to "earn" the title of "Fastest Fat Man in School."

In an effort to spur a big turnout, the university also promoted another first, according to the November 18, 1922, edition of the *IDS*—they encouraged "dates" for the event. As stated in the *IDS* report, "Never before have 'dates' at athletic mixups been smiled upon by the powers that be. The slogan suggested for today is: 'Bring your date and 70 cents—send the band to Purdue.'" Ultimately four hundred people attended, $95 was raised, and the band went to West Lafayette.

★ ★ ★

While Pyle might be the most famous manager who has been involved with IU Athletics, and football might have been the most demanding of the positions in the early years of IU athletics, the tradition and success of the men's basketball team has made their manager's books arguably the most fascinating.

And as is the case with football, the first men's basketball book—one from the 1922–23 season—is littered with fascinating nuggets.

One such item is the fact that the original basketball manager's book—one compiled by senior manager Harold W. Hammond—was lost long ago. Its disappearance didn't come as a result of an accidental purge years later, but happened shortly after the conclusion of the 1923 season. In its place is the book compiled by junior manager W. E. Keisker, which explains in its initial book summary that Hammond's book had been "lost or misplaced," and that the "only one that could be found" was the one assembled by Keisker.

While Keisker's account wasn't intended to be the book of record for the season, it isn't lacking in detail. Its contents include not only the results, statistics, and newspaper clippings from the season, but also obscure information about the selection of halftime entertainment for home games and the financials down to the penny for the team's road trips.

The book's initial pages also include information about the expectations of the fans to show support for the team and for the players to abide by a list of rules designed to produce a championship squad under first-year coach Leslie Mann.

Some of Mann's rules are what one might expect. There was a mandatory team meeting at 3 p.m. Monday through Saturday during the season. Even the inclusion of a team rule barring the use of tobacco in any form wasn't that far off the norm for the era.

But a couple of the other rules?

Rule 3—No eating candy.

Rule 4—No drinking of cocoa (*sic*) cola, soft drinks, etc.

Rule 6—No drinking of coffee.

Rule 7—In bed by 10:30 p.m.

Those four items, along with the team meeting, the prohibited use of tobacco, and a requirement to eat meals at regular hours, comprised the team's seven regulations. Later in the season, Mann added another rule for good measure, forbidding his players from going on any dates during the season. Monitoring the players' adherence to the team rules was the responsibility of not only the coaching staff but the student body as a whole.

"The students can make or break a championship team by not insisting upon every member of a team, now basketball, conforming to the rules and regulations of the team," the 1922–23 team rules said.

The consequences for a violation of these rules weren't spelled out, but Keisker's account made it clear Mann's discipline would be severe. "The player that cheats, sneaks around and breaks training is a traitor, is a man without honor and respect," the rules stated. "He would falter in the pinch for Indiana and therefore ought to be, and will be, dealt with accordingly."

Mann's disciplinary style wasn't exclusive to the basketball team. He was also the baseball program's head coach in 1924,

BASKETBALL RULES.

The following rules and regulations for the Indiana University basketball team of 1922-23 are here published so the students will know what is expected of the players. There should be a happy cooperation between the students body as a whole, and coaches. The students can make or break a championship team by not insisting upon every member of a team, now basketball, conforming to the rules and regulations of the team. It is for Indiana University you are doing deeds and if you would have a winner, you must show your honor, respect, and enthusiasm for the success of basketball. The basketball team will respond to all you ask. Habits regularly adopted aid physical condition far better than training spasmodically. An athlete never should not, to a marked degree, ever break training. He may relax and perform less strenuous activity, but at no time should he stop exercising completely.

Following is a list of the regulations for the team.

1. A meeting of the entire squad each day at 3 P. M. (Except Sunday)
2. Regular hours for meals. No eating between meals.
3. No eating candy.
4. No drinking of cocoa cola, soft drinks, etc.
5. No smoking or use of tobacco in any form.
6. No drinking of coffee or alcohol in any form.
7. In bed by 10:30 P. M.

The player that cheats, sneaks around and breaks training, is a traitor, is a man without honor or respect. He would falter in the pinch for Indiana and therefore ought to be, and will be, dealt with accordingly.

The members of the Varsity squad that are expected to live up to the above rules are:

1. Bahr.	9. Knoy.	17. Weiss.
2. Aldridge.	10. Alward.	18. Marxson.
3. Sanford.	11. Crowe.	19. Champ.
4. Sykes.	12. Eberhart.	20. Minese.
5. Woodward.	13. Crane.	21. Moemow.
6. Coffey.	14. Thomas.	22. Swarmstead.
7. Parker.	15. Sloate.	23. Kilty.
8. Harvey.	16. Yoars.	

and he had a different set of rules for that squad, according to the senior manager H. H. Meyer's account in the 1924 book.

1. No cigarettes. Cigars or pipes to be smoked only in the confines of their respective rooms.
2. Avoid pool halls.
3. Avoid promiscuous swearing.

Mann's no-nonsense approach seemed to filter down to the managers as well. At the start of the 1924 baseball manager's book, senior manager H. H. Meyers includes a stern message to his fellow managers as the season approached.

In an effort to guarantee the 1922–23 Indiana men's basketball team abided by his team rules, basketball coach Leslie Mann called on the IU student body to keep a watchful eye on his 23-member team.
Photo courtesy of Indiana University Archives.

In all caps, Meyers wrote, "DO NOT GO TO COACH MAN [SIC] WITH A LOT OF TRIFLING QUESTIONS. HE HAS PLENTY ON HIS MIND AND CANNOT BE BOTHERED WITH SMALL DETAILS. COME TO ME AND IF I CAN'T SETTLE IT I WILL SEE HIM PERSONALLY."

One of the reasons Mann may have had plenty on his mind was the fact he was not only slated to be coaching three IU teams (he was also an assistant football coach and couldn't assume the men's basketball coaching duties in 1922 until December when his obligations with the football team wrapped up), but his coaching career was only a part-time endeavor. Those two years in Bloomington came in the middle of sixteen-year major league baseball career that ran from 1913 to 1928 and included stints with the Boston Braves, Chicago White Sox, Chicago Cubs, St. Louis Cardinals, Cincinnati Reds, and New York Giants.

During his baseball playing career, Mann played in two World Series (1914 and 1918) and famously turned in an ex-teammate, Phil Douglas, after Douglas wrote a letter offering to accept a bribe to quit his current New York Giants team to help Mann's St. Louis Cardinals squad in their pursuit of the 1922 National League pennant. Mann declined the offer, the Giants went on to win the National League pennant and the World Series that season, and Douglas was subsequently banned from baseball for life by Major League Baseball commissioner Kennesaw Landis.

Mann and the Cardinals, meanwhile, wrapped up their 1922 season with a 7–1 win over the Chicago Cubs on Sunday, October 1, in Chicago and failed to make the playoffs. By Tuesday, October 3, he was in Bloomington and serving on the football coaching staff.

While Mann's stint in Bloomington was only two years, and he's best known for his exploits as a major league baseball player, he had visions of having a lasting impact on the game of college basketball before he departed Bloomington.

The 1924 basketball manager's book includes a press clipping from the March 22, 1924, *IDS*, which details a rule Mann drew up and proposed for adoption in the Western Conference regarding free throws. Mann's proposed rule change was designed to negate a team gaining an advantage due to their height. With the backing of IU Athletic Director E. O. Stiehm, Mann wanted the ball to be ruled dead on free throws; if the attempt was missed, the ball would be returned to center court for a jump ball.

"Basketball is a game of science, and it doesn't look to me as if there is any science in a tall man batting the ball into the basket after a free throw is missed," Mann said in the *IDS* account. "The size of a man should not designate whether he is a good player or not, but rather his headwork, passing ability and accuracy at the basket should be taken into consideration."

* * *

While those early football, basketball, and baseball manager's books detail the exploits of the Hoosier teams, coaches, and players, there is a trio of baseball manager's books from the

1940s that include interesting facts about not only the Hoosier baseball team but also the Cincinnati Reds.

From 1923 to 2008, the Cincinnati Reds held spring training in Florida every year except for three—1943 to 1945. During those three seasons, the nearby professional baseball team instead opted to train in Bloomington at both Jordan Field and, when weather required it, the Wildermuth Gymnasium (now the HPER building on Seventh Street).

The decision to come to Bloomington was necessitated by a directive issued by the US Office of Defense Transportation. With the nation in the midst of World War II, major league baseball teams weren't allowed to travel further south than the Ohio and Potomac Rivers for spring training.

At the time, the Reds were the third most southern team in major league baseball, bested by only the St. Louis Browns and the St. Louis Cardinals. Considering that the Reds' home ballpark, Crosley Field, was less than three miles north of the Ohio River, the Reds had no options for traveling south in March. So they instead opted to travel 130 miles west to Bloomington.

Approval of their stay in Bloomington is detailed in the archived history of the 1943 season. A letter from then Indiana University president Herman B Wells to IU Executive Committee secretary Thomas A. Cookson confirms the Executive Committee's approval in January of 1943 for both the Reds and the Indianapolis Indians to use IU's facilities for their spring training.

While the 1943 baseball manager's book doesn't chronicle the entirety of the Reds' stay—their spring training went from March 15 to April 10 and they were lodged at the Graham Hotel (now called Graham Plaza on the corner of College Avenue and Sixth Street)—it does include details on two highly anticipated spring training games.

On April 7, the Reds were scheduled to face the Indianapolis Indians at Jordan Field, followed two days later by a matchup against the Chicago Cubs (who were holding their spring

training in French Lick, IN) on the Indiana University campus. An *IDS* preview of the games noted the charge for the former was fifty cents and the latter seventy-five cents. Those fees would be waived, though, for "holders of public, faculty and student yearbooks," which could be brought to Jordan Field to secure free admittance. The excitement created by the presence of two professional baseball teams helped offset the struggles of the IU baseball team to not only field a team, but also schedule games. While an *IDS* story shows that Coach Paul "Pooch" Harrell's team had thirty-five players when spring workouts began, multiple accounts noted the prospects of losing players throughout the season to the draft, which had been expanded to males ages 18–37 in December of 1942 via an executive order from President Franklin D. Roosevelt.

Preseason travel restrictions were placed on all major league baseball teams during the latter stages of World War II, prompting the Cincinnati Reds to hold their spring training in Bloomington from 1943 to 1945.
Photo courtesy of Indiana University Archives.

With nearly two hundred thousand males being drafted into the military monthly, Indiana and other teams struggled to field teams and schedule games. Ultimately, Indiana finished 4-1, with the season beginning on March 31 and ending with a rainout against Wabash on April 20—just three weeks later.

The 1943 manager's book noted, following the listing of the team's results, "All Big Ten games and the non-conference games, excepting the five recorded above, were cancelled because of war conditions."

Despite that abbreviated IU baseball season, the Reds' presence in Bloomington in the spring for three years certainly created some opportunities for a couple of Hoosiers to be seen—and ultimately sign with—the nearby professional baseball squad.

Former Hoosier baseball player Ted Kluszewski (*back row, middle*) was first noticed by the Reds in the spring of 1945 while they were training in Bloomington. Kluszewski spent fifteen years in the majors—including eleven with the Reds—and was inducted into the Cincinnati Reds' Hall of Fame in 1962.

Photo courtesy of Indiana University Archives.

Kermit Wahl, a Hoosier third baseman from 1942 to 1944, signed a contract with the Cincinnati Reds in June of 1944 at the Graham Hotel in downtown Bloomington. He reported to the Reds in mid-June, saw his first major league action later that month, and was the Reds' opening-day shortstop in 1945. While it was a promising start to his pro career, Wahl ultimately bounced between the major and minor league levels for the next eleven years, being used primarily as a utility infielder. He hit .226 in 231 major league games during stints with the Reds, Philadelphia Athletics, and St. Louis Browns.

Wahl was the first Hoosier to parlay the Reds' presence locally into a professional opportunity, but the best known Hoosier-turned-Redleg was Ted Kluszewski.

Kluszewski arrived at IU in the summer of 1944, two years after graduating from Argo (IL) High School. Football, though, was the sport that had attracted him to Bloomington. He spent two seasons as a standout end for Coach Bo McMillin's football team, including the Hoosiers' undefeated 1945 season.

Kluszewski played baseball for the Hoosiers in 1945 and 1946, but legend has it that it was his play during spring drills in 1945 that caught the attention of the Reds. Kluszewski's 1988 *New York Times* obituary says he "drew the Reds' attention because he was hitting line drives that broke through a wooden outfield fence" at Jordan Field while the Reds were in town for spring training. Other accounts suggest that after the Reds concluded each day's spring training drills in 1945, members of

the Reds' staff would watch the Hoosiers practice. They would then witness Kluszewski launch batting practice home runs that traveled distances that eclipsed anything that any of the Reds' players could produce.

"Big Klu" ultimately signed with the Reds in 1946, and spent eleven of his fifteen major league seasons in Cincinnati. A four-time National League All-Star, he led the majors in both home runs (49) and runs batted in (141) in 1954, and his 279 career home runs still rank sixth on the Reds' all-time list.

★ ★ ★

While these manager's books serve as a reminder about historical Hoosiers that many know well—like Pyle and Kluszewski—the big names are only a small part of what make these books special.

They also have plenty more. Such as:

⚯ A story of a baseball player who didn't take kindly to criticism directed at his teammates. During the 1924 season, an issue of the *IDS* included a letter to the editor written by Hoosier leadoff hitter Dorsey Kight, who took exception to an editorial written days earlier about teammates Earl Moomaw and Walter Wichterman by the paper's sports editor.

"Here an incompetent and unknown would-be sports editor has been allowed to use the university's press medium to proclaim publicly these men as 'fightless, spiritless, spineless, careless and slovenly outfits, ludicrous to strangers and embarrassing to supporters,'" Kight wrote. "All this comes from a person whose baseball articles have been more or less inaccurate and which have exposed his amazing ignorance of baseball terminology."

"Yet he is allowed to injure the good reputation of two worthy men and athletes who can never be able to defend themselves in the many places where he spread such slanderous lies."

⚯ Financial details that reveal an era long since passed. In 1924, the Hoosier men's basketball team made six road trips—to Lexington, Kentucky; Columbus, Ohio; Urbana, Illinois; Iowa City, Iowa; Chicago; and Lafayette, Indiana. Total expenditures for those six trips was $1,721. The trip to Chicago included a two-night stay at a luxury resort hotel at the time, the Chicago Beach Hotel, which overlooked Lake Michigan. The cost for two nights for thirteen players, which included four meals apiece? $141.75. That was extremely pricey compared to the team's stay in Columbus, Ohio, where twelve people enjoyed a night's stay and a combined thirty-six meals for $58.95.

≈ Among the hard-to-find event programs from the past is one from the Good Counsel Holy Name Society of Newark, New Jersey, dated 1936. They presented the Fortieth Annual National Senior Cross Country Run championship, which featured one of the more remarkable feats in IU team sports history. In a time before the NCAA began holding a cross country championship, IU won the team event at the highly prestigious national AAU (Amateur Athletic Union) event with a perfect score of 15. Led by 1936 Olympian Don Lash (who won three National AAU championships in his career), IU runners finished first, second, third, fourth, and sixth to win the team competition over the likes of the Millrose Athletic Association (which had won the previous seven national AAU titles), the Newark Athletic Club, the Shanahan Athletic Club, and Manhattan College, among others.

≈ Speaking of Lash, the 1936 cross country manager's book includes details of Lash's trip to Germany for the 1936 Summer Olympics in Berlin. That trip almost didn't happen, as the Amateur Athletic Union led an effort for a US boycott of the games in response to reports of persecution of Jewish athletes by Adolph Hitler. That effort narrowly failed. Ultimately, Lash and a team of 334 men and women departed New York on the *S. S. Manhattan* and arrived in Germany eight days later. A July 15, 1936, United Press report that appeared in the Fort Wayne newspaper said Lash and his US teammates would be treated to "a simple diet of beef, vegetables and potatoes until they get to Germany," and that they would also get "a big red apple at 9 a.m. every morning." The US Olympic committee also brought the equivalent of 32,000 glasses of milk on the voyage, along with 1,600 pounds of peanut brittle.

≈ The mode of transportation in the early days was almost always the railway, and a good portion of the Hoosiers' travel expenditures were for Monon Railroad tickets and meals. Hoosier teams would board the Monon and either

INDIANA UNIVERSITY
BLOOMINGTON, INDIANA

EXPENSE ACCOUNT FOR TWELVE MEMBERS OF BASKETBALL TEAM TO COLUMBUS,
OHIO, DETROIT, MICHIGAN AND ANN ARBOR, MICHIGAN. FEBRUARY 15th, 16th
17th, 18th and 19th.

Taxi Friday morning	
Bus for 5 to Indianapolis	$ 1.00
Bus for 7 to Indianapolis	6.25
Pullman to Columbus from Indianapolis	10.50
12 dinners at Station	13.53
11 dinners on train	11.85
Taxi to station at Col. in re Pullman	21.00
Pullman to Detroit from Col.	.75
Taxi in return to hotel	47.25
	.75
Hotel, 36 meals, cab and telephone	58.95
Twelve meals after Ohio-State Indiana game	13.20
Hotel at Detroit, 48 meals, telephone etc.	80.90
Street car fare in Detroit 66¢ Hotel to Station	.36
Milk Chocolate for team	1.20
Hotel, and 12 meals at Ann Arbor	37.25
12 meals after Michigan-Indiana game	8.24
Taxi from Hotel to Station in Ann Arbor 12@50¢	6.00
Pullman Ann Arbor to Chicago	44.25
12 breakfasts at Chi enroute to B'ton	11.30
Street care fare at Ann Arbor, station to Hotel 12@5¢	.60
Taxi-Columbus, hotel to Coleseum and back, twice	16.45
Twelve dinners on Monon diner enroute to B'ton	20.65
Fare for driver of Marmon test car to convey five	
members of the Indiana Basketball Team into Ind-	
ianapolis after smash-up in bus.	2.00
TOTAL --	$416.43

Received from Bursar $450.00
Returned to Bursar   33.57
                          $450.00 $450.00

Signed_____
          Manager

Approved_____
          Director of Athletics.

Railroad fare 371.40

travel to their destination or head to Indianapolis or Louisville and catch a connecting railway. The 1924 men's basketball team, though, had a change of plans, as stated in their manager's travel log: "We were scheduled to leave Bloomington at 11:36 but due to a wreck on the Monon we discovered that we could not make connections at Limedale so we chartered two busses to take to Indianapolis. The two busses left at twelve o'clock. There were five in the first bus and seven in the last. I was in the first bus and we were going at a great rate of speed when due to the fact the brakes were bad and we had no horn our driver crashed into a Ford. We were pretty badly wrecked and nine miles from Indianapolis so I made arrangements with a man testing Marmon sedans to take us to the street car line."

In addition to player biographies, team results, and newspaper clippings, the manager's books also include a variety of other interesting items reflecting nearly one hundred years ago, including travel expense reports.

Photo courtesy of Indiana University Archives.

≈ In many cases, the managers included their own personal narratives about the players' performances during the course of the season, along with additional notes about coaches and staff. Among the more interesting from the very early days:

- Bud Whitlock, equipment manager of the '22 football squad: "Bud appears upon the scene of action every day that the weather will permit and takes care of the footballs and equipment like an old hen takes care of her chickens."
- Max Lorber, member of the 1924 men's basketball team, who was originally listed at 4'11" and then upped to 5'3": "He was the best little man that ever played basketball at Indiana. Smart, clever and a born fighter."

Facing top, The 1923–1924 basketball team. In the back row far left is coach Leslie Mann, and Max Lorber is in the front row, second from the left. *Po020343, IU Archives.*

Facing bottom, The 1926–1927 basketball team. This image was scanned from the 1926-1927 basketball manager's book. Arthur Beckner is in the front row, second from the left. *Po046626, IU Archives.*

- Arthur Beckner, a member of the 1924 men's basketball team: "Although this is Arthur's first year in conference competition, he certainly displayed the cleverest floor work of any man on the team. As one writer said it, 'Beckner on the basketball floor is like Grange on the football field.'"

This is just a snippet of the hundreds of books and thousands of articles and artifacts that make up Indiana Athletics' manager's books, and these types of manager's comments and quips, as well as the interesting stories contained in the books, could go on and on.

These books provide the most thorough retelling of IU sports history from 1922 well into the 1950s, and it comes as a great source of relief to Crabb to know that they're now being preserved in a way to guarantee they'll be around for future generations to reference, consume, and enjoy.

"They're heirlooms of history," Crabb says. "We have to be careful with maintaining them so we have a record of where we've been and from where we came."

Too Many to Name on Wall of Fame

Pete DiPrimio

Jerry Yeagley drives the golf cart. Of course he does. He arrives a few minutes after the start of Indiana University's season-opening soccer practice and everything is waiting for him.

As it should.

Yeagley has earned the right through a Hall of Fame coaching career that resonates as strongly now as it did when he began an improbable success story more than half a century ago.

Late summer finds the Hoosiers launching their annual quest for another national title run, and Yeagley aims the cart for the shade near the side of the practice field, which is a few steps from Jerry Yeagley Field, part of Bill Armstrong Stadium, the home of the Hoosiers' difference-making program.

Yeagley built a powerhouse where none should have existed. He created a dynasty no one saw coming.

But he believed. His assistant coaches believed. Players believed.

And so he watches and contemplates the fruit of all that labor.

Retirement hasn't diminished Yeagley's passion. He remains involved, and even if it's just as an observer of son Todd Yeagley's coaching direction, he embraces it.

A life's work is never really over.

"I can't put that into words," Yeagley says about the pride in building such a program. "It's part of my DNA. Each era, each class, is special in its own way. It reflects the family aspect we've carried on. If you played here, you always will be part of the IU soccer family."

He pauses. A few yards away, players drill under his son's guidance just as they once did under him.

It's the circle of soccer life, Yeagley style.

"It's that unique mystique of IU soccer," the father says.

On this sun-splashed afternoon, signs of mystique are everywhere you look, and where you don't. The banners from

After filling the walls of former head coach Jerry Yeagley's office with All-America plaques that date back to 1974, Indiana soccer had to move the more recent honorees to the team's video room.

Photo by John C. Decker.

eight national titles (the most by any team since 1973), fourteen Big Ten regular season championships, and twelve conference tourney crowns showcase unprecedented success amid a tree-lined Bill Armstrong Stadium setting.

But if you look deeper, if you go behind the scenes and away from the crowds, if you head to the Cream'n' Crimson soccer office wedged into an upper level corner of Assembly Hall, you will see a clear sign of why the Hoosiers have been so good for so long.

It's soccer's Wall of Fame, which is actually three walls covering two offices where sixty-five All-America plaques were displayed in the fall of 2017, with more coming. "I don't know that it was planned," Yeagley says. "It just happened.

When we moved into that office, we didn't have that many
All-Americans, so we put them on the wall. We kept adding
to it."

IU's impressive talent run shows no signs of ending under
Todd Yeagley. The latest earning All-America honors, in 2016,
is back Grant Lillard after his defense-matters junior season.

The plaques tell Jerry Yeagley's story—and so many more.

Forty players earned those sixty-five plaques, starting with
Tom Redmond in 1974. The back arrived as a junior college
player and made an instant impact with his defense. He added
7 goals and 2 assists as a junior, 6 goals and 4 assists as a senior.

In his first season, Redmond led the defensive-minded
Hoosiers, just a year after gaining varsity status, to the NCAA
tourney with a 14-3 record, including 8 shutouts.

And then IU really got good.

The plaques are part of the proof, and you'd bet that Jerry
Yeagley took recruiting advantage. "I felt it was a big extra
touch," he says. "It was an advantage. It was the awe factor. The

pride in the uniform. Here are the greats. Here is the tradition. These are the people, the pioneers who made it possible."

How did it become possible?

What are some of the stories behind all those plaques?

Let's take a look:

★ ★ ★

The All-America names generate memories of Cream'n' Crimson soccer glory. For instance,

Angelo DiBernardo

John Stollmeyer

Ken Snow

Armando Betancourt

Brian Maisonneuve

Nick Garcia
Danny O'Rourke
Mike Freitag
Pat Noonan
Aleksey Korol
Lazo Alavanja
Scott Coufal

DiBernardo was IU's first true superstar. He won the 1978 Hermann Trophy, which goes to college soccer's best player. He was a two-time All-American and a two-time Olympian. He also made *Soccer America*'s All-Century team in 2000. DiBernardo, a midfielder, scored 54 goals and 125 points in three seasons before turn-ing pro. He was a big reason why IU compiled a 53-5-2 record during his playing days, including a 23-2 mark and a national runner-up finish in 1978.

Jerry Yeagley's first All-American was Tom Redmond, who earned the award in 1974—just one year after the sport gained varsity status at IU. Redmond helped lead the Hoosiers to a 14–3 record and the program's first-ever NCAA Tournament berth.

Photo by John C. Decker.

Snow set a Cream'n' Crimson scoring standard that might never be broken. In four seasons, this forward had 84 goals and 196 points, both Hoosier records and an additional school record of 28 goals as a freshman. He also was IU's first four-time All-American and twice won the Hermann Trophy. Like DiBernardo, he made *Soccer America*'s All-Century team. Snow played on IU's 1988 national title team. He helped the Hoosiers to a 73-12-4 record.

Stollmeyer, a midfielder, was a three-time All-American good enough to make *Soccer America*'s All-Decade Team for the 1980s. In four seasons he totaled 27 goals and 93 points. He played in the 1988 Olympics and for the US's 1990 World Cup team. Stollmeyer was part of one of the most memorable games in NCAA tourney history, an eight-overtime IU win over Duke

for the 1982 national championship. That was Indiana's first national title.

Betancourt was the Hoosiers' first three-time All-American and the 1981 Hermann Trophy winner. In three seasons, the forward scored 64 goals and 165 points. He scored at least 50 points three times. He, too, made *Soccer America*'s All-Century team.

Garcia rates as perhaps the best defensive player in NCAA history. Although a gifted offensive player, he took on a defensive back role for the Hoosiers, and the result was national titles in 1998 and 1999. He earned All-America honors in each of his three seasons before turning pro. IU allowed just 39 goals during his 73 career games. The Hoosiers won 67 of those games.

Maisonneuve, who became a long-time IU assistant coach, won the 1994 Hermann Trophy. The midfielder was a two-time

All-American, and won a pair of Big Ten MVP awards. He totaled 44 goals and 110 points in four seasons as the Hoosiers went 75-9-5. He went on to play nine years in major league soccer. He also played in the 1996 Olympics and the 1998 World Cup. As a coach, he was on Indiana's 2012 national title squad and the 2017 national runners-up.

O'Rourke, a midfielder, was the 2004 Hermann Trophy winner, and was a catalyst for IU's national title-winning teams in 2003 and 2004. The Hoosiers also won four Big Ten championships and made three College Cup appearances during his time in Bloomington. He was also an excellent student, and won the National Soccer Coaches Association of America Scholar Athlete Award in 2004.

Freitag, a back, built a four-year career on defense. He was an All-American as a senior in 1979, when the Hoosiers unleashed perhaps the greatest defensive performance in NCAA history. They allowed just 6 goals in 23 games and recorded 18 shutouts. They finished 19-2-2 after spending most of the regular season ranked no. 1.

Freitag went on to become a long-time assistant coach under Jerry Yeagley, and took over the program in 2004 after Yeagley retired. He won a national title and two Big Ten coach-of-the-year awards. He posted an 86-32-19 record in six years as the Hoosiers' coach.

Korol was *Soccer America*'s national player of the year in 1999, the same year he was named an All-American. The forward totaled 149 career points and was named to *Soccer America*'s All-Decade team for the 1990s.

Noonan, a forward, was a three-time All-American and the 2002 Hermann Trophy runner-up. He was twice named

Big Ten player of the year. He helped IU make three College Cups and finished with 127 career points.

Alavanja, a midfielder, was a three-time All-American from 1996 to 1998. He was twice named Big Ten player of the year.

Coufal set the school record for most wins by an IU goalkeeper, with 66. He totaled eight shutouts in 1993, 14 in 1994 and 8.5 in 1995.

Finally, there's **Todd Yeagley**, who was a four-time All-American as a midfielder, who totaled 29 goals and 98 points. He won the 1994 Missouri Athletic Club national player of the year award, and Indiana went 75-9-5 in his four seasons.

No Hoosier appreciates the plaques and what they represent more than Todd, who grew up watching many of those All-Americans.

"For me, when I look at those plaques, it's like I'm reliving my childhood," Todd says. "You're talking about the glory days of youth heroes. I watched players like Angelo DiBernado, Armando Betancourt, George Perry, Mike Freitag, and Dave Shelton."

When Todd was in elementary and middle school, he not only would go to some of IU's practices, he'd participate.

In limited doses, of course.

"I was running around watching them. The stuff Armando could do, to visualize it, that was neat. To see a John Stollmeyer compete, to watch that competitive nature, I'd never seen that. I'd never been around that. I would jump in occasionally when they worked out. Just did little fun things with them. They would kick me up and down. There was no mercy. That showed me what it took. I never had an older brother so they

were like that for me. They beat me up in a good way. They wanted to toughen me up. It was a quick welcome to the big leagues."

* * *

To understand the Wall and what it represents means understanding the kind of players it took to win big at the highest levels. It went way beyond physical talent. In other words, what was a Jerry Yeagley player?

"It was more from the club days when we had to play harder and smarter and defend better than our opponents," the elder Yeagley says. "We couldn't match other teams in terms of technical ability or raw talent. I never let go of that aspect of the game. We wanted to make sure the other teams couldn't play the way they wanted to play. We took them out of their game because we made them work harder. We were more disciplined and we were tougher."

For the elder Yeagley, it started with defense.

"We really focused on individual and team defending. It did give us an edge as we got more talent. We still worked hard. I still think defense wins championships. I look at our teams that won championships. You look at the scores, and it's not the teams that scored the most that won, it's the teams that give up the fewest goals and defended the best. I don't want to take anything away from the offense. I like the beautiful game. I like to play the beautiful game. If you have the talent to do it, you focus 100 percent of the time on offense when you have the ball. But many teams, when they don't have the ball, they don't focus 100 percent. And we did. In transition and defending, we wanted just as much focus there as when we were in possession of the ball and on the attack."

The younger Yeagley has continued that approach even as he has widened the recruiting net. IU goes national when necessary to land title-winning talent.

In 2017 that produced a ten-player newcomer class ranked fourth nationally by Top Drawer Soccer. It included players from Colorado, Massachusetts, New Jersey, and Minnesota as well as Indiana and Ohio.

"The recruiting philosophy has stayed somewhat similar," Todd says. "It's been a four-hour radius of the Midwest. The heart and soul of our team is from St. Louis, Chicago, Ohio, down into Kentucky, and Michigan. We have branched out to the coasts and other pockets where there is interest. Everyone has gotten better, and better players are out there. Our brand is well known. It was back when my father coached, but because of social media, it's easier for a kid in California to see that Indiana soccer has the most national championships. They can see that. They can visualize it. When we make contact, it's easier for them to say, 'Oh, I know about Indiana'. And with our other athletic programs having success—it's great for all of us. It opens doors for all of us."

That IU success includes the baseball team making the College World Series in 2013 and swimmers such as Lilly King winning Olympic gold in 2016.

"We had a couple of break-through performances with some other sports," Todd says. "The college World Series in baseball. Basketball in the Sweet 16 (in 2016). Swimming and diving has been killing it. It's more word of mouth. Now they see it in front of them. That's why we have a Griffin Dorsey from Denver or a Justin Rennicks from Boston (from the freshman class of 2017). We've had kids from those areas before, but it's a bit easier now to get progress rolling."

Ultimately, it's getting the right fit, Todd says. "Our mix of that has always been a strength—a star and a role. Maybe a player is more talented, but he won't fit as well as what we have. Talent is just one part of the equation. It has to be applied. There are a lot of talented under-achieving kids. If we don't think a talented kid would thrive in this environment, we'll take a pass.

"We don't always get it right, but the formula has been successful to find those unpolished, driven kids who just go. It might take two or three years into it before it pays off. We like that hidden gem, a player that has the right mentality and has the tools. It just has to be refined and get into a platform with really good players around him."

And then the younger Yeagley gets to the heart of IU's success.

"The star of our team is never a player. It's always the team. There might be a statistical star or a positional player earning accolades, but that's never the star of the team. That's not the way we've been built."

* * *

Jerry Yeagley arrived in Bloomington in 1963 with a dream. He had been part of a national championship team at West

Chester in 1961. He knew what it took to win at the highest levels. Indiana didn't have it. There was no varsity program. There was no field, no goals, and no university commitment. There was a club team that had been around in some form since 1947.

Mostly it was a bunch of guys playing around after classes. Yeagley changed that.

He taught physical education classes and served as the club team supervisor while working on his postgraduate degree. He had no money for coaching salary, scholarships, team travel expenses, recruiting, uniforms, or basically anything. He and his wife, Marilyn, did everything but cut the players' hair, and even that was negotiable.

The goal was to stay a couple of years and move on.

Then the goal changed.

Finding players was a big challenge. While soccer at the time was popular on the East Coast and in areas such as St. Louis and Chicago, it was virtually nonexistent in the state of Indiana. Add the club sport element and Yeagley had to get creative.

"In the club days, it was guys who were good athletes in the PE classes I taught. We had a lot of international players. Maybe half the team was undergraduate internationals."

That changed in 1973, when soccer became a varsity sport. Yeagley finally had the resources to build a powerhouse.

It started with recruiting.

"When we became varsity and had scholarship help, then I went to St. Louis and Chicago," Yeagley says. "Those were the hotbeds I went to. I felt we could compete there."

Competing came with limits. St. Louis University was the nation's top soccer program at the time. A newcomer such as IU wasn't much of a recruiting threat.

At first.

"Until we had success," Yeagley says, "I would have to get the B-level player, a late bloomer who I thought [top programs like St. Louis] weren't recruiting. Try to develop them. We also went after junior college kids. As we had success and could compete and beat teams like St. Louis, then we could go after the A player, the blue chipper."

There was another challenge. Most elite programs have strong in-state talent to draw from. IU didn't. Not in the 1970s and 1980s. Basketball ruled in Indiana. In a lot of ways, soccer was as foreign as fields of pineapples.

The Indiana High School Athletic Association didn't sponsor a state tourney soccer series until 1994, twenty-one years after it became an official sport at IU, twelve years after the Hoosiers won their first national championship. Youth development was less than ideal. Participation was inconsistent. As a result, there were few elite in-state recruits to choose from.

"Early on, in-state players were support players," Jerry says.

That changed as the state made soccer development a point of emphasis with the national academy program that draws and trains top prospects. IU's 2012 national title team featured seventeen in-state players.

Yeagley points to the 1976 Hoosier team that went 18-1-1 and finished second in the nation as the program catalyst.

"I'd say making the Final Four in 1976, four years after we became varsity, was a crucial turning point in terms of elevated scholarships so we could offer more. Now we could say we could play with the best. We made the Final Four. That was a crucial time."

After that, the Hoosiers became a Final Four—in soccer, it's called the College Cup—regular.

Entering the 2018 season, they had made a record 19 College Cups. Virginia was next with 12. They also led in NCAA tourney appearances (42) and NCAA tourney victories (88).

All that history matters only if you're aware of it. Todd Yeagley likes to see how aware his players are. In August of

Jerry Yeagley capped his thirty-one-year varsity coaching career in 2003 by claiming his sixth NCAA championship with a 2–1 win over St. John's. Yeagley finished his coaching career with an NCAA Division I record 544 wins, 16 trips to the College Cup, and 12 berths in the NCAA championship match.

Photo courtesy of Indiana University Athletics.

2017, during a team meeting the day before official practice began, he tested them.

"We put them in groups and had them answer fifteen to twenty questions of things dating from the 1960s and '70s, to current. Many of the questions were tough.... They answered it as a group. It wasn't about who got it right or wrong, but about starting a dialogue. It was like, 'Wow, this guy did that. That team did this'...We wanted it to stick with them."

And so it has.

* * *

Jerry Yeagley started the Wall of Fame. His son has no intention of ending it.

"The All-Americans is what recruits see when they come into the head coach's office, which is a tradition my father started many years ago," Todd says. "It's not meant to be intimidating, but to show that a lot of great players have worn the Indiana jersey before. To be part of this is a big deal and a big responsibility."

To reinforce that, the younger Yeagley often brings in standouts from the past to talk to the current team. "Whenever we can, we bring them in to address the history of the program in the right context. It's important. They have to know where we started, and why these core values were established, and why they're still important today."

Why they are important is reflected in an iconic Bloomington *Herald-Times* photograph by Jeremy Hogan. It shows a coat-wearing Jerry Yeagley atop his players' shoulders, arms

outstretched in celebration, flashing a beaming smile, in the cold
and snowy aftermath of winning the national championship in
the last game he ever coached.

It was December of 2003. Indiana beat St. John's 2–1 in
Columbus, Ohio.

It was the elder Yeagley's sixth national title. IU had won
two more by the fall of 2017, and the goal is, as always, to win
more.

The Wall of Fame remains a recruiting key to that. "We
give [recruits] information on the number of All-Americans
we've had," Todd says. "That's the biggest thing about coming
to a storied program. It's a reason why we've had continued
success. We've had good players. They want to play with each
other. They want to be pushed. They want to have the competitive nature of what we have."

The Wall draws players. It also pushes them away. That's a good thing.

"It tells players that are intimidated by that environment that maybe it's too much for them," Todd says. "That's okay. We want the ones who want to come and leave a mark here."

For now, the plaques remain in the Assembly Hall office. Eventually they will be moved to a renovated Armstrong Stadium that will include the soccer equivalent of basketball's Cook Hall. More than just plaques will be displayed.

As IU's success grew, so did the number of trophies and honors. There wasn't enough room for them in Assembly Hall, but there was in the Yeagley home. Those are displayed there, and they reflect club successes as well as varsity glory.

Like the plaques, that tradition is carried on by Todd, who owns his parents' former home.

"In our house," the father says, "we had a chronological history starting from the first club team picture up to all the key happenings in the program's history. I got a kick out of taking recruits and parents down there."

And so it continues. "It all stayed," Jerry says. "That's where the recruits go. This is IU soccer history. These are the greats. These are the moments. It's quite something."

Beyond that is the truth behind every great program:

It's about the players and not the honors or numbers.

"The big reward for me," Jerry says, "is to get a call, and I probably get one every day or a text or a message from a former player. Those are the rewards when a kid calls and asks how I'm doing, and says how proud he is to be part of the program. We helped them in soccer and other ways."

He peers from the golf cart. The players work, just as they always have. Energy and purpose are everywhere you look. In less than a week, IU will have its first exhibition. In sixteen days, it will open its season. There is the promise of a much-needed stadium upgrade and the optimism over another championship run.

"I take a lot of pride in the individuals who played here and what the program stands for," Jerry says.

The Wall of Fame reflects that and more.

National Icons, IU Afterthoughts

John C. Decker

7

Can the long-term success or failure of a college football program be determined by one decision?

What about by one letter?

If that is in fact the case, Indiana Football's one-hundred-plus years of struggles might be traced to June 28, 1914. It was then that first-year Hoosier football coach Clarence (C. C.) Childs penned a four-paragraph note to Indiana University president William L. Bryan.

Childs was set to take over the Hoosier program, which had gone a more-than-respectable 35-26-3 during the last nine years under James Sheldon. Childs had starred in the sport while completing his law degree at Yale and upon graduating from the Ivy League school in 1912, began a short-lived coaching career at Wooster (Ohio) College and then IU.

In the one-page letter, Childs informed Bryan that his Wooster College obligations were complete, and he intended to report to Bloomington on August 1. Most noteworthy, though, was Childs's reference to a person who had been mentioned as the possible assistant coach on his Hoosier staff.

"It has been suggested to me that a Mr. Rockne of Notre Dame assist in foot ball next year," Childs wrote. "For several reasons I am not in favor of this plan."

Mr. Rockne was Knute Rockne, who would ultimately go on to compile a 105-12-5 record in thirteen seasons as Notre Dame's head coach from 1918 to 1930. Five of Rockne's teams went undefeated, three were honored as national champions, and Rockne would become one of the most recognized coaching names in the history of college football.

When Childs wrote about his concerns in his 1914 letter, Rockne had just completed his playing career with Notre Dame the previous fall, and was looking for an opportunity to begin his coaching career—potentially in Bloomington. If Rockne were to come to Bloomington, Childs wrote to Bryan, he would "take medicine at Indiana," suggesting Rockne would take classes geared toward a medical degree.

Wooster, Ohio, June 28, 1914.

Dr. William L. Bryan,
President of Indiana University,
Bloomington, Indiana.

Dear Mr. Bryan:

My duties at Wooster are finished and I am now free to take up affairs pertaining to my work with Indiana.

It has been suggested to me that a Mr. Rockne of Notre Dame assist in foot ball next year. He is to take medicine at Indiana in this event. For several reasons I am not in favor of this plan. It has been my intention to interest the Alumni as far as possible this coming season, and I am sure that the methods of Notre Dame are quite different than those of Indiana or Yale. If you think that this particular third system will be beneficial to the athletic life at Indiana next year I will be glad to assist in carrying out your judgment.

Owing to the fact that I was not with you last year, it seems best that I report at Bloomington the first of August. I am asking for your opinion of this arrangement.

Mrs. Childs and I regret that we have been unable to see your Relative here. Pastors of the Presbyterian churches have not found her with the information I gave. Perhaps I mistook the name which I understood as Moore.

Sincerely,

C. C. Childs

But Childs made it clear that if the decision was his (he also served as IU's athletic director during his two seasons at IU), he didn't see Rockne as a good fit. "It has been my intention to interest the Alumni as far as possible this coming season, and I am sure that the methods of Notre Dame are quite different than those of Indiana or Yale," Childs wrote.

While Childs doesn't elaborate on Notre Dame's "methods," the Hoosier coach is most likely referring to a new offensive strategy recently utilized by the Fighting Irish—the forward pass.

While the forward pass is a necessity in today's game, that wasn't the case in the early twentieth century. In fact, it wasn't legalized by the College Football Rules Committee until 1906, a move that came in large part at the urging of President Theodore Roosevelt. A series of gridiron deaths prompted many to call for abolishing the sport, and Roosevelt thought the forward pass would make the game safer. Despite its introduction, an initial series of archaic rules (including one that gave the other team the ball if a forward pass went untouched while falling incomplete) resulted in it rarely being used in the early years of its arrival to the game.

That started to change, though, thanks to several rules changes that made an unsuccessful forward pass less punitive and the November 1, 1913, matchup between Notre Dame and undefeated Army. Notre Dame quarterback Charley "Gus" Dorais completed 14 of 17 passes for 243 yards to lead the underdog Irish to a 35–13 win. Many of those passes went to Rockne, a senior end who had worked with Dorais on the

Prior to the start of the 1914 IU football season, first-year coach C. C. Childs wrote a letter to IU president William L. Bryan in which he made it clear he did not want to hire Knute Rockne as his assistant coach. Rockne would go on to win three national titles at Notre Dame.

Photo courtesy of Indiana University Archives.

forward pass the previous summer while both were lifeguards on the shores of Lake Erie in Sandusky, Ohio.

That win capped a 7-0 season for the Irish and was a landmark victory for the program that struggled to be recognized at the same competitive level of East Coast powerhouse programs such as Army, Harvard, Princeton, Pennsylvania, and Yale—Childs's alma mater.

The success of the forward pass against the high-powered US Military Academy squad in that game convinced many around the country that the play could be a regular part of an offensive attack and not simply a gadget or trick play. But Childs didn't appear to be one of them, preferring the more traditional run-dominated approach that had helped Yale go 125-11-12 from 1900 to 1913.

While there's no record of Bryan's response to Childs's letter, Indiana didn't hire Rockne as its assistant coach during the 1914 season. Childs's Hoosier teams went 6-7-1 overall and 2-7 against Western Conference (now called Big Ten) foes in his two years before he departed to serve in World War I.

Rockne, meanwhile, joined Coach Jesse Harper's Notre Dame staff as assistant coach in the fall of 1914. He spent four years an assistant coach under Harper before taking over as head coach in 1918. After going 3-1-2 in his first season, Rockne led the Irish to their first national title in 1919 and lost more than one game only twice in his thirteen years with the school.

Childs, though, can't be held entirely responsible for the decision not to pursue Rockne as a member of his staff. While he expressed his preferences to Bryan, he also made it clear in his letter that he could be overruled. "If you think that the particular third system will be beneficial to the athletic life at Indiana next year I will be glad to assist in carrying out your judgment," Childs wrote to Bryan.

So if the situation had played out differently, could Indiana have replaced Notre Dame as one of college football's iconic programs? While hindsight might suggest no single decision did more damage to the Hoosier program than this one, longtime IU media relations director Kit Klingelhoffer isn't so sure.

A native of Aurora, Indiana, Klingelhoffer has been a fan of the Hoosiers his entire life and was an employee of IU Athletics for forty-two years before his retirement in 2012. During his time with IU Athletics, he worked closely with numerous Hoosier football coaches, most notably Bill Mallory and Lee Corso.

While he was a first-hand witness to successful seasons (particularly under Mallory) and is well versed in earlier successful campaigns (such as Bo McMillin's undefeated 1945 squad), he's not so sure that even Rockne could have built the foundation for sustained success at IU. "I have seen a lot of IU football history, and in one-hundred-plus years there have been only two winning eras in football here," Klingelhoffer said. "Indiana never started as a football power, and my best guess is [Rockne] would have had the same struggles that every other coach has had."

The reasons for those never-ending struggles, according to Klingelhoffer, are plentiful. The root cause, though, is that the sport of basketball is part of the state's DNA, and football isn't. "It was always a basketball state first," Klingelhoffer said. "When I grew up, football was an afterthought for every kid. It was basketball first, football second, and I don't think that was unique to Aurora High School. Kids who could play both thought of themselves as basketball players, not football players."

That, in turn, has usually resulted in a crop of Division I–caliber high school football players that doesn't rival other states in terms of quantity. When there's an elite, locally produced player, meanwhile, Indiana must not only recruit against other in-state schools such as Purdue and Notre Dame, but also neighboring powerhouses Ohio State and Michigan.

The end result has been a 476-664-45 record in 132 years of competition for Indiana Football, and a 206-486-24 mark in conference games. The 42.0 winning percentage overall and 30.4 success rate in league games are easily the worst among long-standing members of the conference, including that of the University of Chicago, which dropped football in 1939 after going 24-49-8 (7-37-2 Big Ten) during the 1930s.

"What does that tell you?" Klingelhoffer said.

To him, it suggests that even if Childs had wanted Rockne, or if Bryan had overruled his coach's decision, Indiana football would be, well, Indiana football.

"Do I think our football fortunes would be drastically different? No, I don't," Klingelhoffer said.

While Childs missed on hiring one of the most successful coaches in the history of college football, two years later he did manage to attract arguably the greatest athlete of all time to Bloomington. That person, though, wasn't a player who suited up for the Hoosiers. Instead, it was a coach who worked alongside him during the 1915 season.

That coach was Jim Thorpe.

* * *

Who was Jim Thorpe? Probably the greatest American male athlete of the twentieth century.

When the Associated Press polled 393 sportswriters in 1950 about the greatest male athlete of the first fifty years of the twentieth century, the Native American from Prague, Oklahoma, won in a landslide. He received 252 first-place votes, easily outdistancing Babe Ruth's 86 and Jack Dempsey's 19. By the time similar end-of-the-century polling was done,

The winner of the decathlon and pentathlon at the 1912 Olympics in Stockholm, Sweden, Jim Thorpe is considered one of the greatest athletes in the country's history. In addition to his Olympic accomplishments, he was also a Hall of Fame football player and played professional baseball.

Photo courtesy of Indiana University Arbutus.

James Thorpe

Page Seventy-One

Thorpe had all but disappeared from the public's conscious-
ness and although he often finished in the top ten, he fell behind
contemporary athletes such as Michael Jordan and Muhammad
Ali as well as others such as Ruth that he had easily eclipsed fifty
years earlier.

Klingelhoffer certainly knew of Thorpe and his athletic
accomplishments, but he's not surprised that today's sports fan

doesn't share that knowledge. "This generation doesn't know Jim Thorpe," Klingelhoffer said. "I bet if you went on [IU's] campus right now and asked people who Jim Thorpe was, not one person would know. I bet you could ask most IU professors and they wouldn't know."

No matter how he's remembered—or not remembered—in 1915, he had no equal.

In football, Thorpe played for legendary coach Glenn "Pop" Warner at Carlisle Indian Industrial School in Pennsylvania and was a two-time All-American. A punter, kicker, halfback, and defensive back, Thorpe nearly single-handedly lifted Carlisle from obscurity to national relevance. During his All-America seasons of 1911 and 1912, Carlisle went a combined 23-2-1 while outscoring its foes 752–169. The best remembered of those games was one of the most famous upsets in college football history—Thorpe kicked four field goals to help Carlisle upend defending national champion Harvard 18–15 in 1911, ending Harvard's chances of back-to-back national titles.

How dominant was Harvard at that time? Not only did the Crimson win the 1910 national title, but the 1912 and 1913 crowns as well. Harvard went a combined 26-0-1 during those three championship seasons, and after the loss to Carlisle went 33 straight games until their next loss in 1915.

Thorpe would eventually go on to play football professionally for the Canton Bulldogs and then for a number of National Football League teams once it was founded in 1920, serving as the league's first president. He's a member of both the College Football and Pro Football Halls of Fame.

As remarkable as those accomplishments in football were, his exploits in track were even greater. In the 1912 Olympics in Stockholm, Sweden, Thorpe won gold medals in both the decathlon and pentathlon and held the moniker of world's greatest athlete. He won four of the five events to easily win gold in the pentathlon and then proceeded to win four more events while setting an Olympic record of 8,412 points while winning gold in the decathlon.

It was at those Olympic Games where Thorpe met Childs, a fellow member of the US track team who captured a bronze medal in the hammer throw.

Like Rockne, Thorpe wasn't a member of Childs's first Hoosier staff in 1914, but he did join Childs's squad early in the 1915 season. Records suggest Childs first approached the IU administration about adding Thorpe to his staff in early September.

On September 1, Childs wrote a letter to IU secretary Ulysses Howe Smith on the subject. After beginning the letter by citing Smith's previous instructions to him "not to spend a cent this season before consultation," he inquired about the possibility of adding Thorpe to his staff. "I am trying to bring Jim Thorpe the world's greatest athlete here if it is within reason and your judgment," Childs wrote. "It might be well to keep this quiet for the time being. Nothing will be done until you are seen."

One day later, Childs sent a telegram to Smith, advising him that Thorpe would agree to join the Indiana staff so long as IU would pay him $1,000 and provide him and his family with a hotel room. A little more than an hour later, Childs sent another telegram, this one to Indiana University president William L. Bryan, looking for his consent.

"Positive to have James Thorpe Worlds Greatest Athletic assist in football," Childs's telegram said. "Your position is mine. Kindly advise."

Both Smith and Bryan gave their consent to the salary as well as a hotel room at the Hotel Bowles (now called the Graham Plaza), and Thorpe was set to join the Hoosier staff. His arrival, though, was delayed by his own professional sporting endeavors. This time, though, it wasn't football or track, but rather baseball that put his Bloomington debut on hold.

Below, Hoosier football coach C. C. Childs's telegram to Indiana University president Dr. William L. Bryan, seeking his approval to hire Olympic hero and football standout Jim Thorpe as his assistant coach for the 1915 season.

Photo courtesy of Indiana University Archives.

Facing, This receipt stub confirms the amount Thorpe was paid for his stint as the Hoosiers' assistant football coach—$1,000. While there was some talk of Thorpe returning in 1916 to help with football and to coach the IU baseball team, Thorpe left Bloomington in late November of 1915 and didn't return the following fall.

Photo courtesy of Indiana University Archives.

WESTERN UNION TELEGRAM

RECEIVED AT   38DCO 22   4 EX

BLOOMINGTON, IND, 12 28 P.M. SEPT 2

DR. WILLIAM LOWE BRYAN,

BOULDER, COLO,

POSITIVE TO HAVE JAMES THORPE WORLDS GREATEST ATHLETIC ASSIST IN FOOTBALL YOUR POSITION IS NONE KINDLY ADVISE COLLECT.

C.C.CHILDS, HEAD COACH OF FOOTBALL.

11 31 A.M

In 1915, Thorpe was playing professional baseball and was a part of the New York Giants organization. Thorpe bounced between the minors and majors that season, which was the norm for him throughout a career that spanned from 1913

No. 1798   NOV 3 ? ?15 $ 15.62

To James Thorpe

For Trip to Champaign
as scout to see the
Northwestern football game

Balance brought forward	2094 31
Amount deposited	
Total	
Amount of this check	15 62
Balance carried forward	2078 69

No. 1799   NOV 30 1915 $ 1,000.

To James Thorpe

For Salary in full $

for football season
19

Balance brought forward	2078 69

to 1919. That commitment prevented Thorpe from joining Childs's staff until the Giants' season came to a close in early October.

He missed the team's preseason camp as well as the season-opening win over DePauw before his much-celebrated arrival October 7. He immediately began coaching the team's halfbacks and kickers and provided some halftime entertainment for onlookers as well with some punting exhibitions.

While his presence attracted a great deal of interest on campus (the 1916 Indiana University *Arbutus* yearbook noted that Thorpe's "coming to town was a greater event even than Foundation Day is to a Freshman, and the Bloomington schoolboys were more in their glory than when a circus comes to town") and off campus when IU went on the road, his impact on IU's success was negligible. The Hoosiers finished 3-3-1, and the season concluded with a 7–0 shutout loss to Purdue.

Shortly after that November 20, 1915, loss to Purdue, Thorpe headed to West Lafayette, where he played in a game with the Pine Village professional football team against a group of Purdue All-Stars on Thanksgiving weekend. Soon after returning to Bloomington following that contest, he left town again, this time for good. He returned to Oklahoma until the spring when he departed for spring training in Texas with the New York Giants.

Thorpe ultimately spent less than two months in Bloomington, and was well compensated for his time on the staff (in addition to the free housing, his $1,000 salary easily eclipsed the average annual salary of $673 in 1915). But according to Klingelhoffer, it's still remarkable to think that the era's premiere football player and track athlete needed to find work as an assistant football coach in an effort to make ends meet. "It was such a different time—I'm sure he didn't have any endorsement deals," Klingelhoffer said. "It was probably no different than when I was growing up [in the 1950s and 1960s]."

Klingelhoffer noted that during his childhood, it was the norm for major league baseball players to find jobs in the off-season to supplement their baseball income. The better-known players collected fees for making public appearances, while others might need to sell cars—whatever it took to pay the bills until the next season began. "There was hardly a player that didn't have a job [in the off-season] because they were making $10,000 per year," Klingelhoffer said. "That was the 1950s and 1960s, so you can imagine what it was like in 1915."

Left to right, IU assistant football coach Jim Thorpe, unknown individual, IU football captain Frank Berkett Whitaker, *Indiana Daily Student* editor Ralph G. Hastings, IU football coach Clarence C. Childs, unknown individual, November 20, 1915. *P0021916, IU Archives.*

Thorpe's foray into college football coaching was short-lived, and he turned his attention back to professional sports after his departure from IU. He continued his professional baseball career until 1919, playing with the Giants, Cincinnati Reds, and Boston Braves organizations. A lifetime .252 hitter who played in 289 career MLB games, Thorpe's best season was in 1917 when he played in 103 games and hit .237 with 4 home runs, 40 RBIs and 12 stolen bases.

While his baseball numbers and accomplishments were pedestrian at best, professional football was a different story. Before the start of the 1916 season, he signed a contract to play with the pre-NFL Canton Bulldogs for $250 per game. Thorpe led the team to unofficial world championships in 1916, 1917, and 1919, serving as the team's halfback, kicker, punter, and head coach.

When the American Professional Football Association (later renamed the National Football League) formed in 1920, Thorpe not only played for Canton, but was the league's first president. He went on to play for a number of teams, all but one of which has long since vanished from the NFL—Canton (1920), Cleveland Indians (1921), Marion Oorang Indians (1922–23), Rock Island Independents (1924), Rock Island and New York Giants (1925), Canton (1926), and Chicago Cardinals (1927).

While there aren't video highlights or even many statistics from that era to provide evidence of Thorpe's abilities, in the 1950 Associated Press polling of the decade's first fifty years, he was selected as the nation's best football player in the first half of the twentieth century.

After his retirement as an athlete in his early forties, Thorpe struggled professionally and personally. He dabbled in the movie industry during the 1930s and 1940s, although always in minor roles. He was divorced twice, struggled with alcoholism, and when he died of heart failure at the age of sixty-five in 1953, he was virtually penniless.

While his later years were difficult, they can't erase the significance of his accomplishments as an athlete and the fascinating fact that he spent time as an assistant coach at IU—as short-lived as it might have been.

"It's pretty amazing he was here," Klingelhoffer says. "It's a great nugget about Indiana football."

* * *

Speaking of well-known people who spent a brief time in Bloomington...

Have you heard of Harvey Yeary?

Most likely not. After all, he spent only two nondescript years on the Hoosier football team after a standout prep career at Middlesboro (KY) High School from 1957 to 1958. In 1959, he transferred to Eastern Kentucky State University after being expelled by IU for his involvement in a fight at a fraternity party. Once at Eastern Kentucky, he played briefly before a back injury prompted him to quit the sport.

So, if you haven't heard of Yeary, how about Lee Majors?

Now there's a name that most everyone knows. Best known for his TV roles in *The Big Valley* (1965–69), *The Six Million Dollar Man* (1974–78), and *The Fall Guy* (1981–86), Majors was also in the spotlight thanks to a ten-year marriage to fellow 1970s Hollywood star Farrah Fawcett. Majors was presented with a star on the Hollywood Walk of Fame in 1984, and the seventy-eight-year-old continues to play various TV roles to this day.

So what's the correlation between Harvey Yeary and Lee Majors?

They're one and the same.

It was the fight that resulted in Yeary's exit from the Hoosier program, and it was his arrival in Hollywood that prompted Yeary to shed his given name for "Lee Majors."

How did Harvey Yeary become Lee Majors? According to former Hoosier player and coach and current IU Assistant Athletic Director Mark Deal, it had a football twist to it. "Lee

was Harvey's middle name, and Majors was the name of Harvey's favorite football player, Johnny Majors," Deal said. "So he took his own middle name and the last name of his favorite player and became Lee Majors."

Johnny Majors was a star at the nearby University of Tennessee during Yeary's high school career, winning the Southeastern Conference's Player of the Year award in both 1955 and 1956. While Yeary was putting together a senior season in 1956 that earned him an IU scholarship, Majors was the Heisman Trophy runner-up that same season after guiding the Volunteers to a 10-1 record by totaling 1,001 yards and 12 touchdowns.

Yeary had visions of emulating his childhood hero on the football field, which clearly didn't materialize. But after giving up his job as a parks and recreation director in North Hollywood Park, California, to pursue an acting career in the 1960s, he blossomed into a pop culture icon, someone whose celebrity quickly rivaled and then eclipsed the former University of Tennessee player and coach.

Like Jim Thorpe and Knute Rockne, Yeary's impact on Indiana University football was little more than a footnote. But the lifetime accomplishments of all three, either on the football field or off, still make their tangential affiliation with the program worthy of note.

"Those are three pretty well-known people affiliated with Indiana football," Klingelhoffer said. "I'm sure in each case I was stunned when I first heard their stories. I can remember with Thorpe, when I first heard it, I thought the person who told me was crazy.

"Turns out it was true."

All of them were.

Don't Look Down on Assembly Hall

John C. Decker

*Simon Skjodt Assembly Hall has struck fear in many
a person since its doors opened in 1971.*

The reasons are plentiful. One was long-time coach Bob Knight, one of college basketball's most intimidating and imposing figures. His presence for twenty-nine years brought a buzz and a level of drama to every Hoosier basketball game, no matter if IU was among the nation's elite any particular season or not.

Another is the seventeen thousand–plus fans that pack the arena for games religiously, bellowing at foes from courtside and seemingly hovering overhead from the balcony seats.

A third reason is a series of Hoosier players that have been among the nation's best. Since the building opened its doors during the 1971–72 season, it has been the home to twelve Big Ten MVPs, and twenty-five All-Americans have helped IU to three national championships and fourteen Big Ten titles.

But did you know the building can be every bit as frightening when there are no coaches on the sidelines, no players on the court, and no fans in the stands?

★ ★ ★

One can tap into that fear by venturing behind the door no. 199 in the southwest corner of the building, next to the stairs that lead down to court level.

Only a special key, held by only a handful of special people, can get you through that door. What waits isn't a room, but rather sets of stairs, ladders, and handrails that will take you to the upper reaches of Assembly Hall, some 130 feet above the court. Your trip overhead will include journeys across metal grate walkways that provide unsettling views of the court below, leaving you doubting the stability of every step and your own ability to put one foot in front of the other.

It's a trek that will leave the bravest uneasy.

And for those with anything less? White knuckled and crippled with fear.

To ascend to the upper reaches of Simon Skjodt Assembly Hall, one begins their journey up multiple sets of stairs that are located behind the grey Tectum walls on the north and south ends of the arena.

Photo by John C. Decker.

Few have been up there as many times as IU Assistant Athletic Director for Facilities Chuck Crabb. A forty-one-year employee of IU athletics, Crabb has spent the last twenty-seven years overseeing IU Athletics facilities, and he can still remember his first trip to the top of Assembly Hall.

Crabb received a phone call from the house electrician, who needed Crabb to accompany him to "the grid."

The grid is the three-story structure that descends from the copula of Assembly Hall and is directly over the court. Inside the grid, among other things, are the building's air-handling equipment, a large hoist system that holds the 40,000-pound video scoreboard, and a number of abandoned electric motors that were installed when the building was first built to maneuver battens for any theatrical productions held at Assembly Hall.

While Crabb hadn't been up into the grid before this early 1990s trip, he knew very well that it was some 100 feet above the court, and he wasn't enthusiastic about the prospects of the adventure. "I said, 'I don't like heights much,'" Crabb says. "And [the electrician] said, 'Don't worry about it. You'll be fine.'"

So they met outside door no. 199 in Assembly Hall's southwest corner and began their journey.

The first portion was relatively easy. First came two sets of stairs, followed by three fireman's ladders. All of this occurs behind the grey Tectum wall that spectators see on the south end of the arena. A fourth fireman's ladder took the electrician and Crabb to a level that was some 90 feet above the court. They then walked straight ahead into the bottom floor of the grid.

The electrician then flipped a couple of breakers to illuminate the arena while also enlightening Crabb about how high he was as they were able to look directly down over center court. "The visual trick he played on my mind was he had a dark room, so I had no sense of depth perception," Crabb said. "So I didn't know exactly where I was, or that I was 90 feet over the Assembly Hall court. I really liked it."

Crabb didn't like the next suggestion, though.

While standing in the grid is unsettling in that it is approximately 100 feet directly over the court with views down through the metal grating underfoot, it does provide some level of security. You're relatively enclosed within the three-story structure, and you're not subjected to perilous views unless you seek them out.

That isn't the case, though, for the "catwalk."

Extending from the grid above the 10-second half-court line are two cement-pathed, open walkways that lead to sets of arena lights that run parallel to the court on the east and west sides. These walkways are anchored into the cable system that supports the roof, and a trip down the H-pattern path leaves you with an unavoidable, unobstructed, and unnerving view to the court below in every direction.

For the few who have gone to the top of Assembly Hall, this is often where fear foils the final stage of the journey.

"The electrician said, 'Come on Chuckie! We're going out on the catwalk!'" Crabb says. "I was holding on for dear life."

* * *

That's the case for most everyone who ventures to the top of Assembly Hall, particularly during their first handful of trips. When most return to the comfort of solid footing on one of the building's main concourses, they'll reemerge not only with a great story to tell but also covered in perspiration.

That sweat is the result of not only the frightening trip but a hefty dose of heat emitted from the arena lights. "If you go up even in the winter, you're probably going to be in Bermudas and a T-shirt," Crabb says. "Those lights put out a lot of heat."

Those lights are a relatively new set of Musco arena lights that were installed in 2010. In all, there are ninety-six metal halide lights affixed to the catwalk and directed at the court. When those lights were installed in 2010 for approximately $750,000, they represented a marked improvement over the previous lighting system, which included nearly two-and-a-half times as many lights—248

When the Simon Skjodt Assembly Hall court is illuminated, those who travel to the top of the arena are greeted by an unsettling clear view of the playing surface more than 100 feet below.
Photo by John C. Decker.

of them. "When they sold us on the lights [in 2010], they were the best metal halides that they had," Crabb says.

While the new lighting system was a big improvement, like the previous unit, it emits a generous amount of heat. While it might not cause a rise in temperature on the court, it certainly can be felt on the grid—and even more so when venturing onto the catwalk, where sweaty palms aren't welcome.

That extra heat would have likely been avoided if IU had waited even one more year before upgrading the building's lighting system. Shortly after the new lights were installed, a trend began where colleges started installing Musco's LED lighting systems instead of the traditional metal halides. These LED systems—which produce little or no heat from the lighting fixtures—have become the norm thanks to the savings they can offer cost-conscious college athletics departments.

According to Crabb, other athletics departments say they have seen a 70 percent savings on their electric bills with the LED systems compared to what they had been paying. That, coupled with LED rebates from electric providers that can get into the low six figures, enables those with new LED lighting systems to pay off their initial investment in less than five years.

"We got in one year too soon," Crabb says.

So for the foreseeable future, the metal halide lights will remain, and sweating high above will continue.

★ ★ ★

In addition to those metal halide lights, there are a handful of other lights that reside in the upper reaches of Assembly Hall. These lights provide a reason for another group of people to journey above regularly.

Sports photographers have long installed their own temporary lights—or strobes—to provide additional lighting and to improve their ability to capture fast-moving action images at basketball games. These temporary lighting systems are synched to the photographer's camera, illuminating the subject as an image is captured.

Before IU upgraded its lighting system, strobes were almost a must for anyone trying to get high-quality color images. While the original lighting system did include nearly 250 lights, it was from the late 1960s and produced a yellowish hue, which was particularly apparent when shooting color images (instead of black and white, which was much more prevalent in the 1970s and 1980s). In addition to the color issue, the system just didn't produce enough light to allow photographers to shoot at the higher shutter speeds that are best suited for action photography.

For those media outlets that could afford it, temporary strobes were the solution. *Sports Illustrated* was the first to utilize them in Assembly Hall in the late 1980s. Soon afterward, local newspapers that covered Indiana University basketball on a regular basis, such as the *Bloomington Herald Times* and the *Indianapolis Star*, followed suit.

To adequately light the playing surface, media outlets needed four strobe heads directed at the top of the key on each end of the court. The pursuit of these high-quality color sports photos wasn't cheap; according to *Herald Times* photographer Chris Howell, the set of strobes his newspaper still uses—which was originally bought in the early 1990s—cost approximately $25,000 when it was originally purchased. The price of strobe lights has dropped significantly, but a new set would still cost around $8,000 today, Howell says.

The set-up of those temporary lights, meanwhile, is also taxing. Placement of the strobe heads in each of the court's four corners requires installation at each of the four extremities—or corners—of the catwalk system.

Technically, the only people who are supposed to be doing work above the court are members of the International Alliance of Theatrical Stage Employees, Local 618, since it is a union-controlled area. While the IATSE, better known as the Stagehands, do handle the Assembly Hall set-up for events such as graduation, arrangements have been made to allow the photographers to affix their own equipment.

For the handful of photographers using strobes on a regular basis at IU home games, that means not only venturing to the top of the building for the initial installation before the season starts but also return trips before each and every game to turn them back on.

Considering those requirements, there is probably no one who has gone to the top of Assembly Hall more than Howell. Now the director of photography for the *Bloomington Herald Times*, Howell has been photographing Indiana University sports for nineteen years. His first trip to the top of Assembly Hall came when he was interning for the newspaper in 1993, and he's returned hundreds of times since. In the late 1990s, he was entrusted with a key to door no. 199, but the stricter facility security measures that were put in place following 9/11 now require him to get access from IU Athletics staff.

He says if he ever did have a fear of heights, his trips to the top of the building have ended them, but he still realizes it's a journey that will distress most. "My advice for anyone going up there" Howell says, "is to have the respect for it that it deserves. Gravity is not something to be messed with."

For Howell, the impact that gravity can have isn't only about making sure he returns to the main concourse the same way he left it. It's also guaranteeing he doesn't accidentally drop a piece of equipment or personal item from above. That could do damage not only to the item dropped but also the court or anyone below. "Whenever I go up, I'm stuffing everything in my pockets—nothing is in my hands or in a shirt pocket," Howells says. "Ideally when we're up there it's at times when no one is below us, but that isn't always the case. So you're doing everything you can to make sure you're not endangering anybody below you or yourself."

That approach has served him well, as he says he's never accidentally dropped anything onto the court. He says he vaguely remembers another photographer once dropping something, although the name and the item escapes him—either due to a lapse in memory or professional loyalty. "It was something like a lens cap, something minor," Howell says. "I can't remember who it was. I'm sure a lot of people, if it was them, wouldn't admit to it."

Even from 100–130 feet, a plastic lens cap isn't going to damage anything below. But there are items that Howell and other photographers place above the court that could. In addition to the strobe heads and shells, Howell and other photographers, on occasion, mount remote cameras that they can operate from court level.

Since there's nothing to catch the photographers' equipment should it fall, they provide multiple levels of protection.

"The strobe head itself is secured with a professional clamp, and there are metal cables that we run through the strobe head so that, God forbid, the clamp breaks or gave way, we have the redundancy of the cable to hold the strobe head and shell so they don't fall," Howell says.

The same goes for the remote cameras. A relatively small camera weighing approximately 5 pounds would hit the floor at nearly 55 miles per hour with 6,000 pounds of force if dropped from 100 feet. According to Crabb, that's why the rule of thumb is that any rigging that needs to be done before a sporting event must be done in the morning before the game, long before players and spectators fill the arena.

Simon Skjodt Assembly Hall's catwalk is also used by a handful of photographers, who mount strobe lights to the arena's upper reaches to provide enhanced lighting when photographing IU basketball games. *Photo by John C. Decker.*

"There's definitely some liability involved," Crabb says. "It's just too easy for a screwdriver to be dropped, or a wrench, a camera, and suddenly you have a projectile that could easily penetrate the hardwood floor, could penetrate a skull, very, very easily."

Another less-strictly-enforced rule is that no one is above the court when a game is being played and fans are in the stands. But occasional exceptions are made—Howell says an equipment malfunction can require a trip up to reset a unit during a game.

On at least one occasion, he also found himself up top before a game, and saw a picture that he couldn't resist taking. Howell was on the northwest corner of the catwalk, directly above the IU bench, and captured an image of former IU All-American Victor Oladipo as he was introduced—by Crabb—shortly before a game's opening tip. "I probably wasn't supposed to be up there taking that picture, and they certainly knew I did it after they saw it [in the paper]," Howell says. "Maybe they thought I did it with a remote camera, which is ideally the way we'd do it. But I had to go up late, and I wanted to make the picture. So I shot it."

With so many trips to the grid and the catwalk under his belt, Howell said he's not rattled about going up. But he's been up enough times with other people who haven't shared his confidence that he's well aware of the trepidation that the trip can produce.

In his early days with *The Herald Times*, Howell took a photographer from the *Evansville Courier* up when he was doing his pregame routine of turning on the strobes and the receiver along with dropping a cord from the receiver to the floor to connect to his camera. Unaware of his friend's hesitation, Howell led him on a journey up the stairs and ladders and onto the grid. When it was time to venture onto the catwalk to turn everything on, the fellow photographer stopped.

"He put his hands on the wall as I'm talking to him from about five or six feet away," Howell says. "I told him to follow me out and he looked at me and said, 'No, no, no. You go ahead.' I had no idea he was afraid of heights. I've taken a couple of other people up there that have been intrigued by it, and they've ended up frightened by it. It's intimidating up there. I've been up there so many times, but I still realize that."

Like Crabb, it's the catwalk that Howell says is most unsettling. "You'd think the walkway would be metal or something really sturdy," Howells says. "But it's these concrete slabs, laid side by side, with some cracks in them, and really nothing underneath. You start walking around fast up there and you can start feeling the catwalk move a little bit, so that freaks people out."

One reason the catwalk isn't constructed in a more substantive way is the fact it isn't designed to hold a great deal of weight. Since this isn't an area that's accessible to the general public, you won't find any weight limit signs posted before you venture down one of the two paths. But it's safe to say that there won't be any tour groups making their way up there anytime soon.

"The amount of weight is something we've always had to be careful about," Crabb says. "But those are the type of computations that engineers and architects had worked on once upon a time as they put the building together back in 1955 when it was originally designed."

There's little doubt that the appearance of the grid adds an additional level of queasiness for those who venture above the court. Wander around the three-story building and you'll find a random broom that clearly isn't being used, and a stray soda can that has been left behind. There is a miscellaneous folding chair on the lowest level of the grid, as if there's ever a reason for anyone to do anything other than complete the task at hand and retreat to safer surroundings as quickly as possible.

Up until six years ago, Crabb says, you would have also found garden hoses and clear plastic tarps in the grid.

Why?

"From the day Assembly Hall opened in October 1971 until when we put a totally new roof on the building [in 2011], that stupid roof leaked, and it was a royal pain," Crabb says.

The rather rudimentary fix that IU used for nearly forty years to address the issue? IU removed standing water from the building's roof by running garden hoses from it down into the grid and onto the clear plastic tarp placed along on the bottom floor of the grid. Aided by the heat generated by the lights, the water would evaporate. That forty-year fix was no longer needed after the $2 million roof project was completed in 2011, so the hoses and layer of tarp are now things of the past.

With even less need for staff to go up to the grid since the completion of the roof project, the area has become dusty and disheveled. The railings would be things to avoid for cleanliness-conscious visitors if it wasn't for the fact that they're the only things available for those who are looking for something to hold onto for dear life.

While nearly all of the IU Athletics staff works in either Assembly Hall or across the parking lot in Memorial Stadium, very few of those staff members have ever been up to the grid or out onto the catwalk system. They don't necessarily have a reason to be up there, even if it does offer a unique view of the court that won't come from anywhere else in the building. "I'd say that easily 95 percent of the people [who worked in athletics] haven't been up there," Crabb says. "At least."

The same goes for other campus entities who might have work-related concerns with the building, according to Crabb. "Those who work in facilities operations, any of the engineers on staff that work plans and create pathways and know how things need to go, most of them will go up there," Crabb says. "But any of the actual architects? Or any of the bosses, if you will? Ain't going to be any way they're going up there. No way at all."

At the top level of the grid above Simon Skjodt Assembly Hall, one can gain access to the building's roof, which was replaced in 2011.

Photo by John C. Decker.

In addition to the entryway in the southwest corner of the main concourse, there's also a virtually identical route from the northeast corner that will take you behind the Tectum wall on the north end of the court. For the less adventurous, one can also take the arena's north lobby elevator to the top floor and then ascend two more sets of stairs. The right person can then get you through a locked door that will have you at roof level.

However you get there, if you can muster up the courage, and find the right person, a trip to the top is breathtaking and, for most, heart stopping.

"It will scare the be-jimmies out of you," Crabb says. "But wow—what a view."

9

Clear as a Bell How IU Secures the NCAA Track Meet

Pete DiPrimio

Sam Bell did what couldn't be done. Many argued that it shouldn't be done.

Bring the 1997 NCAA track meet to Indiana?

The same Indiana that had perhaps the worst college track and field facility in the country?

Are you nuts?

Coach Bell didn't care. He was a track-and-field force of nature, with twenty-two Big Ten titles and twenty-three top-ten team national finishes on his Hall of Fame resume. That he happened to work at Indiana during the bigger-than-life era of Bob Knight shouldn't diminish his impact and legacy.

He was a man who got things done.

"You didn't discourage Sam Bell for nothing," Harold Mauro says. Mauro had first-hand experience. He's a former IU senior associate athletic director whose responsibilities included overseeing track and field. He worked closely with Bell for years. "Sam felt he was in charge and he ruled the roost," Mauro says. "He was a strong-minded individual who liked to see things done in the correct way, a positive way. I liked coaches like that."

Bell also had a knack for salesmanship. He convinced NCAA officials to award the NCAA meet to Bloomington rather than to Indianapolis, which had Carroll Stadium, one of the top track facilities in the country (and IU's home away from home), or other contenders.

Bell did that even though IU's track surface in the mid-1990s was an injury waiting to happen. The bleachers were, to be polite, unfortunate. There was no real press box or scoreboard or ticket office or adequate concession stands. There was just a mess and a dream, and it was hard to tell where one began and the other ended.

No matter. IU got what it wanted—an opportunity to do something special on a national scale. "We had the desire to show people Indiana track was back in Bloomington rather than in Indianapolis," Assistant Athletic Director Chuck Crabb says. "That's stayed true since then."

Randy Heisler remembers when Bell broke the news.

Heisler was an assistant track coach under Bell in the spring of 1996. He was sitting in the track office with Mauro, Crabb, and fellow assistant coach Marshall Goss waiting for Bell's return. Bell had spent the day in Indianapolis pleading his case to NCAA officials. He was adamant that the meet belonged in the Midwest. More specifically, that it belonged in Bloomington, at Billy Hayes Track, and not in Indianapolis.

For the record, the Hoosiers had hosted the NCAA meet in 1966. It returned to the state in 1986 at Carroll Stadium. The meet was usually held in the West (Oregon was a popular location) or in the South (Texas, Tennessee, and Louisiana were favorite sites).

Bell returned to his Cream'n' Crimson office and everyone expected a rejection story.

"There was no way we were going to get that meet," Heisler says. "No way. There wasn't a snowball's chance in hell."

Sam Bell won twenty-two Big Ten championships in twenty-nine years as the head track and field and cross country coach at Indiana University and was inducted into the USA Track and Field Hall of Fame in 1992.

Photo courtesy of Indiana University Athletics.

Two decades later and he still laughs thinking about it. "We didn't have a facility. We didn't have bleachers. We didn't have a track where you could host a junior high meet without fear of somebody getting hurt by falling into a hole.

"Sam comes back. He walks in the room and says, 'We got it.' We were like, WHAT? Marshall and I were dumbfounded. How did he do that? Harold and Chuck were like, 'Oh, my God. What are we going to do?'"

Given the looming workload and expense, fear and dread made sense. "I was surprised we got the bid in the sense we had a run-down track," Mauro says. "We knew we needed to do some repairs and an upgrade, but our coaches really wanted it from the standpoint of enticing the IHSAA [Indiana High School Athletic Association] to host its state track meets here, which eventually happened."

"It was a big effort. When you put the bid in, you never know if you're going to get it. We didn't think we would because of the condition of our track and the other amenities there. Once we did, the Athletic Department put the ball in motion to enhance the facility."

How did Bell do it?

"Here was his sales pitch," Heisler says. "He walked in and scolded [NCAA officials]. He said there hadn't been an NCAA meet on a college campus in the Midwest in over twenty years. He said there hadn't been one north of the Mason-Dixon Line in ten years, and shame on them. He said, we'll do it and we'll do it right."

Bell could back up such talk with performance. In previous years with Bell in charge, Indianapolis had hosted the Olympic Trials and the Pan Am Games. The execution had been flawless. He was known as one of the best track meet organizers in the country.

"Nobody was going to put on a meet better than Sam Bell," Heisler says. "[NCAA officials] couldn't come back on that."

Getting the bid was one thing. Keeping it was not guaranteed. Not even close.

But first …

* * *

How bad was IU's track facility?

Let's look at the history.

The facility was good enough to host the 1966 NCAA track meet, which UCLA won. Then officials let things slide so that when Heisler arrived as an assistant coach in 1985, "the track was absolutely atrocious. I don't think anything had been done to it since the late 1960s."

The evidence backs up that statement.

"In my first twelve years at Indiana we hosted only one meet in Bloomington, the Billy Hayes Invitational, and only because Sam felt it should be at Billy Hayes Track," Heisler says. "Everything else was in Indianapolis. We hosted everything you could imagine there. It became our home track."

Bell was instrumental in getting a first-class track facility built in Indianapolis. His goal was to do the same thing in Bloomington, and saw the NCAA track meet as a catalyst. If

IU got the bid, it would have to spend the money to upgrade the facilities, which would boost recruiting and more.

That leads back to the earlier question—how bad was IU's track?

"I remember one day telling [IU athletic director] Clarence Doninger, that I will shut up and not complain ever again about the facility if you will let me walk you around our track, if you can walk a full lap blind-folded without falling in a hole," Heisler says. "I told him, 'I'll hold your hand. You'll never leave lane 1 to lane 5'. I mean, there were holes and patches. It was a disaster."

Bell had begun pushing for a facility upgrade in Bloomington in the early 1990s. "A lot of people thought Indianapolis was IU," Heisler says. "We'd hosted the NCAA meet there. We'd hosted the Olympic Trials, the Pan Am Games, the Olympic Fest, and a USA Track and Field meet there. That's where the track meets were and that's the only time they'd come to [the state of] Indiana. They never came to Bloomington."

Bell was ready to put Bloomington back on the track map.

"Coach Bell was adamant—he wasn't going to do anything half-assed," Heisler says. "He was afraid if it didn't get done the way it needed to be done now, it might not ever get done right."

No way Bell would let that happen.

"Sam was that kind of guy," Heisler says. "He was like, 'Why can't we do it? Don't tell me why we can't do it. We're going to do it.'"

So the Hoosiers did.

★ ★ ★

Once IU got the bid, officials had a year to raise the money and get the facility ready to host the nation's premiere college track event.

Yes, there was pressure. "I was really nervous," Mauro says. "I couldn't eat. I lost ten pounds."

When did the pressure end?

"When the meet started. That's when I breathed a sigh of relief."

There was a reason for such stress—IU nearly blew the opportunity because of a lack of money.

In July of 1996, Crabb was in Atlanta observing Olympic preparations, and then the Olympic Games. His job was to see how Olympic officials did things there to prepare IU for the next year. "It was a great experience to see everything in practice before we did it," he says.

He almost wasted the trip. IU officials were considering giving the meet back to the NCAA because they couldn't pay for the upgrades. "We didn't feel we had the facilities that were going to be suitable for hosting the championship," Crabb says.

Then he got a call from Doninger.

"He said, 'Hey, we've got a major gift. We're going to build your stadium'. I could sleep at night after that."

It soon became two major gifts—one from Robert Haugh and the other from the Gladstein family. Haugh contributed $1.5 million. The Gladsteins started with $1 million, then later added to it. The result—the track facility was renamed the Robert C. Haugh Track and Field Complex. The indoor facility was renamed the Gladstein Fieldhouse. The total cost of the outdoor project, including resurfacing the track, was nearly $6 million.

So the money was there. Now came the construction, and challenges were everywhere.

For instance, the hammer throw is an NCAA meet event. At the time, it was not a Big Ten or IU event. There was no place to hold it. "I don't know if Sam concerned himself with minor details like that," Heisler says with a laugh. "I said, 'Coach, these guys throw those things like 250 feet. They can't throw it on the infield. It would ruin the irrigation and ruin the infield.'"

"He said, 'We have a hammer field.' I asked, 'Where?' He pointed to a little spot in the woods north of the track and said, 'They're going to cut all that down and make a new field there.' I was like, 'They're going to cut the forest down?' He said, 'Yes.'"

"I asked Harold Mauro about it. He kind of shook his head. But you know what—it's there. We built one, and a kid set an NCAA record there. It was a great success."

Along the way Heisler got a great educational lesson the Sam Bell way.

"He gave me the job of being head of officials. At the time, you didn't pay officials. Everybody was a volunteer. If you were working a track meet for Sam Bell, for every event you had to have everything specific as far as where they met, where they walked, everything. It was a production. I learned so much from him. It was like, Randy, do this. OK. Randy, do that. OK. I really enjoyed it."

In the week leading up to the meet, the rain came and wouldn't stop. A front had stalled over Indiana, dumping rain at a biblical rate. "I remember the day teams were arriving Harold was in the parking lot with a broom, sweeping off mud and water," Heisler says.

Then the rain stopped and the competition began.

"You know what—it worked out," Heisler says. "It couldn't have been any better."

* * *

For Harold Mauro, it was time to get dirty.

Indiana's senior associate athletic director ditched his tie, his dress shirt, his dress pants, and his dress shoes. He tapped into his inner landscape man. There was an IU track infield to sod, the clock was ticking, and he wasn't about to let the Hoosiers blow it.

So Mauro went to work. He got the Indiana wrestling team to help. He had some clout in that area given another of his responsibilities was overseeing the wrestling program.

"It was a rush at the end," he says. "We had five truckloads of sod coming in two days before the meet. I went to the wrestling room and told them they were going to get in shape with me. We were going to lay sod. I changed my clothes and was out there laying sod on my hands and knees for two days. They did, too. They did a hell of a job. It was really hot. It was tough. They were saying, 'we're glad you're not having any more surfaces replaced or sod put down.'"

Mauro, a member of the IU Athletics Hall of Fame, never shied away from hard work. That was true when he played line-backer and center for the Hoosiers from 1964 to 1967 (including the 1968 Rose Bowl), then when he was an assistant coach for Northwestern and Indiana, then as an IU administrator. Along the way, Mauro was a participant in nine of the Hoosiers' ten bowl games. He also was inducted into the Indiana Football Hall of Fame.

So he was fine with getting dirty. "I always found if you get down and show them you're willing to roll up your sleeves and take your tie off and get dirty with them, they don't mind doing the hard work with you," he says. "I've always been like that."

Mauro fully understood the stakes, and wasn't about to have things go wrong.

In fact, when Bell returned from Indianapolis with the bid secured, Mauro responded with the Cream'n' Crimson equivalent of the win-one-for-the-Gipper speech. "It was like, 'Ok boys, what are we going to do about this? We have a heck of a year ahead of us, and we can't miss a day. Not one day.'"

And in the closing days, when the heavens opened up and stayed open, "We were praying for no rain," Mauro says. "Everyone in the Athletics Department pitched in, even if it wasn't their sport."

Yes, you could see Mauro sweat.

"When you're in charge of a sport, you want to make sure everything runs smoothly, and that the coaches have every-thing they need. That way they only have to worry about coaching. They don't have to worry about if the hurdles will be up or if the surface is going to be OK."

"Well there was a lot to worry about. We had to get the new track surface in. We wanted to plant trees. The entry way had to be done. Ticket booths had to be built. We were tightening bolts on the bleachers at 3 a.m. on the day of the meet. We had to do a double check on everything."

The to-do list had one other thing:

"One of the biggest challenges was how to get the athletes to and from the venue," Mauro says. "We used a wagon pulled by a cart. We took pedestrians and fans as well as athletes. We had a lot of volunteers from the community. And Marshall was over the top as far as organization."

That would be Marshall Goss, then an IU assistant track coach, later the head coach. He got plenty of help from Heisler and others. "The track coaches worked hard to host the meet," Mauro says. "It went extremely well. There were some records set."

In the team races, Arkansas won the men's title for the sixth straight season with 55 points. Texas was second with 42.5. For the women, LSU edged Texas 63–62 for its eleventh straight championship. UCLA was third with 56 points. Arkansas would also win the next two seasons before its streak ended. LSU's streak ended the next year.

"That didn't surprise me," Mauro says about the successful meet. "Indiana has always been very good at putting on events. Guys like Chuck Crabb are real seasoned in doing that."

And then:

"It turned out well. They did a hell of a job."

So well, in fact, that IU embraced hosting other events, including the Big Ten wrestling tourney. "It encouraged other sports to try to get events on our campus," Mauro says. "It's important to host things. The wrestling was a massive undertaking as well. It's a lot of work."

* * *

For Chuck Crabb, it was a time to laugh.

Athletic Director Clarence Doninger had submitted two NCAA meet bids for IU—one for Bloomington, one for Indianapolis. "I joked that we were bidding against ourselves," Crabb says.

Crabb was the assistant athletic director in charge of many things, including facilities. When the Hoosiers won the bid, a large part of the get-it-ready responsibility fell on him. "We knew we had a lot of issues to address," he says. "We needed an appropriate locker rooms area. We needed adequate seating. We needed a fully automated time system. None of those elements were in place."

IU had previously used a track surface that "was basically as hard as North Jordan Avenue," Crabb says. "It was very tough on athletes' shins. We went with the synthetic surface that was used in the Atlanta Olympics in 1996."

The facility had 3,500 permanent seats. Bleachers pushed capacity over 6,000.

After getting the facility ready, running a first-class meet wasn't a problem, Crabb says, given the caliber of people organizing it. "We knew we could do it. We had a team in place of people who had hosted meets through all the years in Indianapolis. We simply brought them down to Bloomington and put the meet on."

"There was nobody who was better at putting on a meet than the late Sam Bell. From the timing to making sure we stayed on schedule to making sure we had full sections of a race or flights in a field event. Everything worked like clockwork."

It's not easy when you have an eighteen-event track meet for men and women, with everything from the 100 meters to distance races to field events. "That can make for a long day," Crabb says. "How well are you able to show results? How well can you track field events? If in the third round of the long jump, somebody jumps into the lead, people need to know that. You don't want a five-ring circus where nobody has any comprehension about what's going on in front of them."

"That's one of the things Sam made sure of. We always had a timing system and reporting equipment that allowed us to stay on top of what was happening."

Bell, who passed away in 2016 at the age of eighty-eight, envisioned developing IU into a Big Ten track powerhouse, both for the men's and the women's programs.

In so many ways, he accomplished that.

He coached 141 Big Ten outdoor individual champions, 92 Big Ten indoor champs, 69 outdoor All-Americans, 63 indoor All-Americans, 15 cross country All-Americans, 11 Olympians (including Bob Kennedy, Jim Spivey, Sunder Nix, and DeDee Nathan) and 2 crosscountry national champions. He also was the US men's distance coach at the 1976 Olympics.

Still, Bell wanted to set the stage for Indiana to do more, and you can't do that without quality athletes, and you can't get them without a quality facility. Using Carroll Stadium helped, but it wasn't ideal. Bell never lost sight of his return-to-Bloomington goal. "It was easy for us to work our schedule and do our competitions at IUPUI and Carroll Stadium," Crabb says, "but Coach Bell was like, 'Let's get rid of that fifty miles and make Hayes Track the showplace that it once was when it first opened in 1966.'"

Meanwhile, there was recruiting to do. Before 1997, Bell and his staff got creative. "Not that you lied to anybody," Heisler says, "but when we took recruits and their families on a tour of the facilities, we'd drive to the cross country course. We'd show them the indoor track. When we went to the outdoor track, we'd have them in a car and drive to the parking lot, then make a quick turn and drive out. As for out-of-state recruits flying into Indianapolis, Heisler says IU coaches would pick them up, "then drive to downtown and show them the [Carroll Stadium] track where we hosted home meets."

After 1997, a new era began. Heisler took over the women's program in 1999 and took full recruiting advantage of the facility upgrade. "Once we put the track in and hosted NCAA, that was a game changer," Heisler says. "We were able to bring in athletes who became NCAA champs and runner-ups.... We

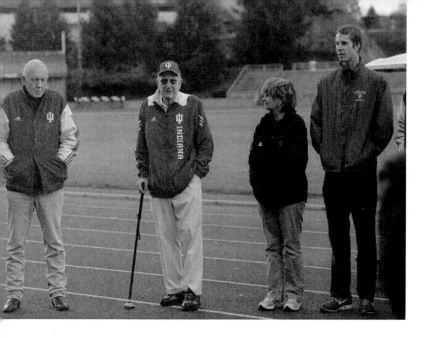

took them down there. Then it was the nicest track in the country. The kids were impressed. They were like, 'Wow.' It showed the dedication the university had to the sport."

It led to a huge recruiting coup—landing the boys' and girls' state track meets. For eighty years, the meets had been held in Indianapolis. From 1983 to 2003, they were held at Indiana University-Purdue University at Indianapolis [IUPUI] and Carroll Stadium.

IU officials wanted to host them. Now that the Hoosiers had a first-class track facility, athletic director Terry Clapacs made a huge push for them. "I found out IUPUI was charging an arm and a leg to the IHSAA [Indiana High School Athletic Association] to host the meets," Heisler says. "I talked to Terry and he was excited about it."

Heisler set up a meeting with Bobby Cox, then an associate IHSAA commissioner in charge of track, now the overall commissioner. "I asked him, 'Have you guys ever considered coming to Bloomington for the meet?'" Heisler says. "He asked me, 'What would it cost?' I said, 'Nothing. We would comply with any NCAA rules, but it will be a minimal financial situation for you. You could have the gate, and we'd get six hundred of the best high school athletes on our campus for two days. You can't pay for that.'"

And so every June since 2004, the state's best boys and girls track athletes come to Robert C. Haugh complex for two days of action. "Without us hosting the NCAAs and getting that upgrade," Heisler adds, "we would never have gotten the high school meets. That was a direct result of having that facility in Bloomington."

* * *

Could IU host another NCAA track meet?

"Why not?" asks Crabb. "We've let [the NCAA] know that we're interested."

Eugene, Oregon, has hosted the meet the previous five years, and has it locked up until 2021. "Texas A&M is putting in a strong bid," Crabb says. "Arkansas would like to host again."

IU's facility remains NCAA ready, with this big exception—seating.

"It takes 8,000 to 12,000 seats to host the NCAA meet," Crabb says. "We could probably do 8,000. Bloomington is the smallest city that tries to get the meet."

Track surfaces need to support speed, be durable, and be safe for the athletes. Harder surfaces work well for sprinters. Softer surfaces aid distance runners. "When you host a meet like the Olympics," Crabb says, "you want harder compression because they're built for people like Usain Bolt to have great 100- and 200-meter times. But if you have them for the 5,000 meters or the 3,000-meter steeplechase, it can be demanding on people's shins and ankles. You have to find a happy medium."

"We always look at our surface. The one we have has been down for eight years. It's lightning fast. We just have to watch

In addition to coaching IU athletes to All-America recognition 147 times, eleven of Bell's Hoosier athletes competed in the Olympics, and he was a member of the US Olympic coaching staff in the 1976 Games in Montreal.

Photo courtesy of Indiana University Department of Athletics.

it every year to make sure it has the right amount of rubber on it and that it's not exposing too much of the sub-surface."

As far as the rest of the stadium, Crabb says, "We still have the original scoreboard from 1997. It uses old incandescent bulbs. That's a technology scoreboard companies don't maintain anymore, so we have to think about what to do there to make sure we have a good system that displays results so people can enjoy what they're seeing. A new scoreboard would cost between $500,000 and $700,000. We're trying to be proactive and not reactive so we can plan ahead.

"This is a very viable facility for practice and hosting championship meets. We look forward to future meets. Who knows? Maybe we can get the NCAA meet back."

If IU does, it can thank Bell, who retired in 1998, a year after the NCAA meet, having seen his vision come true.

The Robert C. Haugh Track & Field Complex at E. C. "Billy" Hayes Track, 2009.

In the end, Mauro said, it was mission accomplished. "I'd say it was at least an A-minus. After it was over, everyone came up and said, 'You put on a hell of a meet. The service was phenomenal. We'd like to come back'. When that happens you feel you've done your homework and your job."

Or, as Heisler puts it, "The place was a swamp. Now it looks like a park."

Somewhere, you figure, Sam Bell is smiling.

What's the Racquet?

John C. Decker

10

Indiana University Athletics' Henke Hall of Champions houses relics from some of the most memorable accomplishments in Hoosier sports.

Many NCAA championship teams and individuals are commemorated, as are past Hoosier Olympians. There are uniforms, game programs, trophies, and mementos that highlight the school's biggest names and teams. Almost all of the items remind Hoosier fans about stories they either personally witnessed or heard about from previous generations.

There is, though, one exception.

There's an encasement that requires a closer look and further explanation. It holds a 1980 Wilson Ultra Graphite tennis racquet and Nike tennis shoes from the same era. The commemorative plaque notes both were used by Heather (Crowe) Conner when she won the AIAW national singles championship and led IU to the 1982 AIAW team title.

Those words elicit three questions from most visitors.

Who's Heather Conner?

What's the AIAW?

Why haven't I ever heard of her or the AIAW before?

* * *

Regarding the first query, Conner is the most accomplished of a plethora of decorated protégés of legendary IU tennis coach Lin Loring. The winningest coach in the history of women's collegiate tennis with 846 wins over the course of forty-four years, Loring recruited Conner when she was a standout junior player from Masconomet High School just outside of Boston in 1980.

At the time, Loring was in just his third season at IU and a long way from being able to pick and choose any player he wanted to bring to Bloomington. Conner, meanwhile, had visions of escaping the cold weather in the Northeast. "Being from Massachusetts and having to play indoors, my goal was to go to a school I could be outdoors all year," Conner said.

But Indiana reached out, and good fortune came Loring's way. As a top-100 national recruit, Loring connected with Conner about visiting his program. While her national ranking put her on IU's radar, the fact that she was ranked in the seventies, according to Loring, helped keep the Hoosiers in contention. "Her ranking was high enough that the Floridas and the Stanfords weren't going after her," said Loring, who retired in early 2017 after forty years at the helm of the IU program. "So we didn't have to compete with them."

Loring convinced Conner to visit the Bloomington campus, and she and her mother made the trip to Bloomington. It was a trip, though, that nearly didn't come to fruition due to a near miss in the airport.

On the final leg of their trip from Boston, they looked at the list of departures for their gate, located one destined for Bloomington, and made their way to the plane. Seated and ready for take-off, the flight attendant announced they were ready to close the doors and depart ... for Bloomington, Illinois. "We freaked out," Conner said. "We jumped up and got out."

They got off the plane, and found the correct flight headed to the Monroe County Airport in Bloomington, Indiana. That flight had its own issues as they traveled on a small plane on a very icy night, but a safe landing and a great visit convinced Conner that Loring and IU were the right fit.

While there have been many better-known accomplishments by Indiana University athletes over the years, Heather Conner's 1982 season—which included a national singles and team championship and a run at the US Open—remains one of the great individual performances ever by an IU athlete.

Photo by John C. Decker.

Loring knew he was getting a good player when Conner committed, but he quickly learned he was getting a great one.

The strengths on the court were quickly obvious. A left-hander, Conner had a good slice serve and was "quick as a cat," Loring said. While she didn't overpower opponents with one big shot, she was excellent at the net and solid on both the forehand and backhand sides. "She didn't have a weakness," Loring said. "You really had to beat her—she didn't beat herself."

Those attributes were enhanced by a work ethic that frankly can't be duplicated these days.

Today, NCAA rules permit student athletes no more than twenty hours per week in competition or practice while they are in season. Such restrictions were nonexistent in the early 1980s, and Conner made every effort to maximize her time on the court.

On Mondays, Wednesdays, and Fridays, she scheduled her classes to start at 7:30 a.m., and on Tuesdays and Thursdays they began at 8 a.m. A business school student, Conner managed to finish her classes before noon each day, giving her the entire afternoon to train. A typical day would involve spending an hour working one-on-one with Loring, departing for an hour, and then returning for the team's afternoon practice.

"I knew she was going to be great because of how hard she worked," Loring said. "With that type of work ethic, I knew the sky was the limit."

She quickly emerged as the team's no. 1 player as a freshman, which was no small feat considering All-Americans Tina McCall and Bev Ramser both returned from the 1979 squad. She was a mainstay at the top of the Hoosiers' lineup for the next four years, ultimately compiling a 130-33 record in singles and a 104-23 mark in doubles. She earned All-Big Ten honors four times, All-America honors twice, and was tabbed as the Big Ten's Player of the Year for three years.

While Conner's accomplishments each season were significant, it was the 1982 season that stands out. After a dominant regular season individually and as a team, Indiana entered the national championship event in Iowa City, Iowa, as one of the team favorites. Loring's squad rolled through the team

competition, ultimately knocking off second-seeded Cal-Berkeley, 6–3, to claim Indiana University's first-ever—and to date only—national women's team championship.

Conner remembers the team celebration at the hotel lounge that evening. "This is 1982, so they had a juke box, and we all went down and were dancing to [Kool and the Gang's] 'Celebration,'" Conner said. "We were all going crazy. But I'm also thinking we're starting the individual competition the next morning."

Conner had visions of adding an individual singles championship to the team title, and was considered one of the top contenders. But the favorite for the title was top-seeded Vickie Nelson from Rollins College. Ultimately, Conner and Nelson met in the final, with Conner winning, 7–5, 6–2.

Thirty-five years removed from that victory, Conner still remembers many of the match's details. She says Nelson wore down opponents with her consistency from the baseline, and Conner knew she had to do something other than try to match her. "I came to the net a lot, tried to rush her," Conner recalls. "I kept the ball low, used a lot of slice, used my left[handed] angles. That was huge."

It was a game plan that was put together in large part by Loring, whom Conner credits a great deal for helping her win that match and the title. "I learned this a lot when I was playing professionally—a coach really can make a big difference," Conner said. "I had some talent and ability, and I was driven and motivated, and all of that is great, but you need all the pieces to come together. He really added that piece, especially in that match. He probably played a bigger role in that match than any match I ever played."

When the match ended, Conner can still remember Loring running out and giving her a hug as they celebrated the individual title to go along with the team crown. "It was awesome and there was definitely some [feelings of] I can't believe it," Conner said.

But it was true—she'd won the national championship. The AIAW national championship.

But what was the AIAW?

* * *

AIAW is an acronym for Association for Intercollegiate Athletics for Women, which was founded in 1971 and was the primary governing body for intercollegiate women's athletics during the 1970s and early 1980s. While the NCAA oversaw men's sports on college campuses, it showed very little interest in being involved with women's sports during that era.

That created an opportunity, one that the AIAW seized for the better part of a decade.

"[The AIAW] was all about opportunity for women," said Mary Ann Rohleder, who served as the IU Athletics senior women's administrator before retiring in 2010. "It was big schools, small schools, it was a come one, come all type of organization."

During the 1970s, women's intercollegiate athletics was in the initial stages of gaining widespread acceptance. Previously, athletic opportunities for females were negligible if not nonexistent on most college campuses. The only avenue was generally via club sports under schools' departments of physical education. At the time, women's teams were very rarely part of the intercollegiate athletics departments.

That began to change in the 1970s, and happened in conjunction with the passage of a critical piece of legislation— the Education Amendments of 1972. That federal law included a component that would ultimately have an immeasurable impact on women's athletics—Title IX.

Title IX stated that "No person in the United States shall, on the basis in sex, be excluded from participation in, be denied the benefits of, or be subjected to discrimination under any education program or activity receiving Federal financial assistance." While the law didn't specifically address the disparity in opportunities in collegiate athletics based on gender, public universities realized it could—and most likely would—be interpreted that way.

As a result, athletics departments slowly began fielding women's sports teams as part of their intercollegiate athletics programs. While there remained a large disparity in terms of scholarships and overall funding for the women's sports relative to the men, it was a significant step in the growth of women's athletics.

The next big change happened in 1979. The federal government's Department of Health, Education, and Welfare (HEW) was fielding a host of complaints alleging gender discrimination by public universities' athletics departments across the country. That prompted the department to release an interpretation of Title IX with regard to how it related to intercollegiate athletics. The interpretation was designed to provide guidance to intercollegiate athletic programs to become compliant with the law. That interpretation, according to Rohleder, is "what really got the ball rolling" for women's sports.

Among the noteworthy items were that athletics departments needed to offer scholarships in a way that was commensurate with the proportion of student athletes by gender. Equal treatment was also required in areas such as equipment, travel, staff salaries, facilities, and support services.

HEW's interpretation made it clear that the days of women's intercollegiate athletics being an afterthought relative to the men's programs were coming to an end.

The impact of that statement would also have consequences for the AIAW.

* * *

Before HEW's interpretation, athletics departments were doing little to provide significant financial support to women's sports, and the NCAA had little interest in having any involvement. But as the tide began to turn, the NCAA started showing interest in offering women's sports championships.

While the NCAA might have expected women's programs to welcome the opportunity to make the switch from the AIAW, that wasn't the case. There were a series of contentious debates on the subject. Oftentimes, athletics directors and university presidents faced stiff resistance from within their own institutions, as women's coaches and newly added women's administrators questioned the motivations and sincerity of the NCAA's newfound interest in women's athletics.

"For the women, it wasn't all about money," Rohleder said. "It was about opportunity. With the NCAA, I think the women were skeptical that now [the NCAA] saw some money in it, wanted that, and also wanted control."

Rohleder and Loring also knew that if the NCAA did begin offering women's championships, they would be in direct competition with the AIAW's tournaments, and the consequences for the AIAW would most likely be dire.

In the end, the NCAA decided it would offer women's championships beginning in the 1981–82 season. In an effort to try to convince schools to compete in the inaugural NCAA women's championship competitions, the governing body hired Occidental College's Ruth Berkey away from the AIAW and tapped her to head its championships events.

In addition to that move, both Loring and Rohleder said the NCAA wasn't shy about strong-arming other important powerbrokers if necessary to enhance its chances of taking control of women's intercollegiate athletics quickly. "The NCAA did a power move," Loring said. "Up until then, the good old boys didn't want a thing to do with women's athletics. Then it became politically correct to support women's athletics. My understanding at the time was the NCAA went to ABC, NBC, and CBS, and said if you give [TV] contracts to the AIAW [to broadcast any of its games], you won't be broadcasting any NCAA Basketball." NBC did cancel its exclusive deal to televise AIAW championship events in 1982, a move that came as the NCAA began offering women's championship events.

Rohleder isn't entirely sure of what tactics the NCAA used to ultimately gain control of women's athletics, but she knows it had plenty of means to influence decision makers at the institutions. "[The NCAA] was very powerful," Rohleder said. "The NCAA had all the power and the AIAW had none. The AIAW was formed out of a need. Then, the NCAA decided it wanted [women's athletics]. I'm not sure of all the hammers it wielded, but it was strong arming the [athletics directors]."

Ultimately, both the NCAA and the AIAW offered women's championship events during the 1981–82 season, and teams could participate in one or both. While many schools did take the opportunity to compete in two national championship events, Indiana's women's tennis program only participated in the AIAW tournament.

That decision came as no disappointment or surprise to Loring.

Leanne Grotke, who had overseen the transition of women's sports at IU moving from the School of Health, Physical Education and Recreation to the Athletics Department, had served as IU's coordinator of women's athletics and director of women's sports from 1972 to 1979. A pioneer in the growth of women's athletics at IU and nationally, she also served as the commissioner of large college championships for the AIAW. That made it a no-brainer which championship Indiana would compete in. "It was kind of understood that we were going to play in the AIAW and not the NCAAs," Loring said.

While the label of *AIAW champion* might not carry the same cachet that *NCAA champion* does in this day and age, Loring says there is no asterisk by either the Hoosiers' team championship or Conner's individual crown. In the team competition, he said, approximately three-quarters of the women's tennis programs competed in both events in 1982.

In the individual competitions, Nelson was the no. 1 seed in both tournaments, and went on to earn a spot in the

Wimbledon field later that summer. "Heather had a lot of good matches at number 1 [in the AIAW team tournament competition] going in, and there isn't a lousy number 1 when you get to nationals," Loring said. "So she was playing some good tennis and was one of the favorites. But it was still an upset. I don't think anyone thought anybody could beat Vickie Nelson."

But Conner did just that, capping a magical season that included a program record of 39 dual match wins to go along with the AIAW individual and team championships.

Ultimately, those would prove to be the final AIAW tennis championships awarded to either a team or individual, as the governing body folded on June 30, 1982. It filed an antitrust lawsuit against the NCAA alleging the NCAA used its monopoly power in men's sports to push the AIAW out of business in women's sports, but it lost the case and ultimately any chance of staying afloat. "The AIAW died overnight," Loring said. "The AIAW went from the only people in town who cared about women's athletics to literally out of business in six months."

Loring understood that in the long run, the move to the NCAA could create new opportunities for women's athletics. But that realization didn't completely offset the disappointment in how it unfolded. "The NCAA was going to bring more resources to the table, but the way it happened was really bad," Loring said. "But it was the good old boys making a power move. They had all the money, and they had the sports that TV really wanted, which was football and basketball."

★ ★ ★

With the death of the AIAW, Indiana began competing in the NCAA championships in 1983. Loring's teams qualified for the NCAA Tennis Championship event twenty-three times, including twelve straight times from 1987 to 1998. Making Loring's run of success even more impressive was that ten of those trips came during the 1983 to 1995 era when the NCAA women's tennis tournament field included only sixteen teams (1983–87) or twenty teams (1988–95).

While his forty-year run at IU was littered with All-America players and magical seasons, no year would ever rival 1982, and no player would ever match Conner in terms of individual success.

Conner's success, meanwhile, didn't end with her AIAW title. First, her national title earned her a spot on the US Junior Federation Cup team. A strong showing on that squad, coupled with some solid results in a handful of summer tournaments, ultimately helped her land a wild card entry into the 1982 US Open.

While the trip to Flushing Meadows, New York, for the year's final Grand Slam event was a significant step up from the competition she'd faced at the collegiate level, Conner said she wasn't intimidated. "There was something inside of me—I was confident," Conner said. "I didn't have any problem once I was in the tournament feeling like I could win anything."

Conner did make some significant noise at the Open. After opening with a 6–1, 6–1 win over Stacy Margolin in the first round, she ousted fellow American Barbara Hallquist 7–6, 1–6, 7–6 to advance to the Round of 32. There, she met sixteenth-seeded Zina Garrison on center court.

After playing in front of little more than family and friends throughout her collegiate career at IU, her match against Garrison took place at the 18,000-seat Louis Armstrong Stadium. And as the match went along, the attendance grew. "The match didn't start with that many in the stands, but as they put the scores up, the crowd kept growing," Conner said. "It was exciting, and I was hyped up. I didn't realize I enjoyed playing in front of a lot of people, but there was an energy that I really enjoyed."

It was a closely contested, back-and-forth match. One point sticks out for Conner more than any other in the third-round matchup. Garrison hit an approach shot to Conner's backhand and followed it into the net. Conner wound up and fired a backhand passing shot for a winner.

But the ball wasn't the only thing headed to Garrison's side of the court. Conner said that when she was frustrated with her play during a match, she had a tendency to hit her racket either on her foot or her leg. She had seen no signs that she had damaged her racket before the passing shot, but in the immediate aftermath of it, she realized she had. "The ball whipped by her, and at the same time my racket split in two," said Conner. "I was still holding the handle after the shot, and the racket was flying up toward her, kind of like a baseball bat breaking. People were clapping and cheering, but it was so embarrassing to have to walk up there and pick up my racket." After that

point, Conner said, things began to slip away, and she eventually lost the third-round match 6–2, 7–5.

While her US Open run came to an end, it was still a remarkable accomplishment for a college player to reach the final 32 at a Grand Slam event. Loring says, to the best of his knowledge, no active college player has equaled that feat since 1982.

After that performance, Conner said she toyed with the idea of not returning to IU, but ultimately decided to put her professional career on hold. "During the summer, I had a lot of offers thrown at me," Conner said. "An agent wanted me to turn pro. Someone else wanted me to transfer to their school on the West Coast. I had all those thoughts in my head, along with whether or not to come back to IU. But I knew getting a good education was important, and I knew once you turn pro, it's not easy to go back and finish. So I thought about it, but I decided to come back and get my degree."

A three-time All-American at IU, Conner's professional career was cut short due to a series of injuries. She did, though, compete in all four majors, highlighted by her run to the round 32 at the 1982 US Open.

Photo courtesy of Indiana University Athletics.

Conner did earn her business degree and after an injury-riddled senior season, turned professional. She climbed as high as no. 223 in the world singles rankings and ninety-sixth in doubles in 1987 before injuries forced her to retire soon afterward.

"I feel a little bad for her because what she did in 1982 is one of the greatest accomplishments by an IU athlete ever that no one really knows about," Loring said. "No one really knew about it because there wasn't the internet or social media. But she was really Lilly King before there was Lilly King."

King, as most sports fans know, won Olympic gold in both the 100-meter breaststroke and the 4 x 100-meter medley relay at the 2016 Olympic Games in Rio shortly after the conclusion of her freshman year at IU. Her performance catapulted her from a relative unknown to one of the best-known swimmers in the world.

While the internet and social media has something to do with that, so does the fact that women's sports enjoy a much greater platform than it did in 1982 when Conner was excelling on a national level without the same fanfare. "It's the nature of the beast—no one cared [in 1982], unfortunately," Rohleder said. "At least no one unless they were directly involved in it. That's too bad, because [Conner's success in 1982] is every bit the accomplishment of anything any other IU athlete has achieved, but no one knows about it."

★ ★ ★

IU Athletics took steps to be sure that people would learn about Conner's accomplishments when it completed its North End Zone Facility in 2009. That project—which involved enclosing the north end of Memorial Stadium—included the construction of the Henke Hall of Champions as a special event location. Featured in it are museum-type pieces from IU's storied past—including Conner's racket and shoes.

Conner said she was contacted by IU Athletics staff when they were assembling memorabilia, and she was flattered. That flattery, though, was offset by a fear that she might not have any souvenirs from her 1982 season. "I didn't have a clue if I had anything, and I'm thinking what am I going to do?" Conner said.

Fortunately, Conner said she's a bit of pack rat, and with a bit of digging, located the racket as well as the shoes hidden away in a cardboard box. "I never had any intention of wearing the shoes or playing with the racket because they were so outdated," Conner said. "I was shocked when I started digging around and found them. I thought they'd be perfect."

IU agreed, and the items are prominently displayed alongside other pieces that tell stories of other great accomplishments by Hoosier athletes and coaches. Conner returned to Bloomington for a 2016 tennis reunion and saw her items on display for the first time, which she admits was special. While her racket and shoes are just one of a number of items on display in the museum space, that type of notoriety felt a bit unusual for an athlete who grew up in a time when there was little or no attention paid to women's athletes or athletics.

"I grew up in an environment when people only went to watch the guys," Conner said. "But that didn't faze me. I felt I was always going to go out and try to do what I was going to do. If no one knew about it, it didn't matter."

It does now.

Gold Standard: Knight Assembles Team to Remember in '84

John C. Decker

Thirty-three years ago, arguably the United States' greatest amateur basketball team was assembled in Bloomington.

The architect of that team was Indiana University head coach Bob Knight. In 1984, Knight was at the forefront of the college basketball scene, thirteen seasons and two national titles into an IU coaching career that would span an additional fifteen seasons and add another national crown. That success made him a logical choice for USA Basketball when it tabbed him to select and coach a team that would play on home soil in the summer of 1984 at the Olympic Games in Los Angeles.

Knight welcomed seventy-three of the country's best amateur basketball players to Bloomington in April of 1984, all fighting for twelve roster spots. Many of those players—some of whom didn't make the team—would eventually become household names. Michael Jordan. Karl Malone. Patrick Ewing. Charles Barkley. John Stockton.

"As the team formed, you could tell it was a pretty special group," says Tim Garl, IU's head men's basketball trainer who served in that same role on the '84 US team. "They bonded, got close, and had fun as a group. But they were also a team on a mission. And coach never let them forget that."

Thirty-three years later, reminders from those trials remain in Bloomington. Indiana University Athletics passed along hundreds if not thousands of action photos from practices and scrimmages to Indiana University Archives. There are also scores of statistical sheets from those same scrimmages, which helped decide the makeup of a team that would eventually win its eight contests at the Los Angeles Games by an average of 32 points on its way to the gold medal.

Perhaps most interesting, though, are a handful of one-page, typewritten sheets with notes on various players. Those notes, according to Garl, are from Knight.

* * *

The numbered comments broke down the player's efforts and performances on both ends of the court, and included anywhere from eighteen to thirty observations on various players who were competing for a spot on the team.

One player's notations included twenty-four comments, all of which were critical. A few of those notes:

By the time Bob Knight was selected to coach the United States' 1984 Olympic team, he had already won two of his three national titles in Bloomington.

Photo courtesy of Indiana University Archives.

"1. Loses sight of ball—Doesn't help on post."

"8. No stance—poor post defense—foolish foul."

"21. Drifts into occupied post instead of popping out to wing for spacing."

Of course, with seventy-three players invited to the trials, there were bound to be some that weren't up to Knight's standards. That must explain these comments about a player, right?

Those were Knight's comments about Michael Jordan, the then-University of North Carolina standout who would go on to win six NBA championships and five league MVPs to lay claim to the moniker of greatest player in the history of the game.

Thoughts on another player:

"3. Kills dribble and can't improve passing angle."

"7. Throws ball to baseline with no purpose."

"20. Doesn't use dribble to take ball to the shooter."

Those comments were about a then little-known guard from Gonzaga—John Stockton—who would go on to become the NBA's all-time leader in assists.

And Knight's take on a third player:

"4. Lack of defensive alertness."

"7. Slow defensive recovery—poor defense to the ball."

"19. Just walks across the lane—doesn't look for screening action to initiate offense."

That player? Georgetown center Patrick Ewing, who would go on to rank in the top twenty-five in NBA history in scoring, rebounding, and blocked shots.

Another player who didn't make the final roster also drew a critical take from Knight:

"3. Poor defensive stance, no passing lane pressure, no testing stance."

"11. Forces a bad shot, has open men post at the free-throw line."

"23. Dribbles into trouble instead of waiting to see if the post man is open coming off the cross screen."

Fresh off leading Georgetown to the 1984 NCAA championship, Patrick Ewing anchored Team USA in the post. He averaged 11.0 points and 5.6 rebounds in the squad's eight Olympic games, with a high of 17 against Uruguay in Pool Play.

Photo courtesy of Indiana University Archives.

Those thoughts were on Auburn forward Charles Barkley, who would go on to earn first- or second-team All-NBA honors ten times and one NBA MVP award.

Finally, a fifth player whose inability to get open offensively drew critical thoughts from Knight:

"1. Drifts—stands—doesn't set up cuts."

"4. Doesn't screen anybody—doesn't make hard cuts to get open."

"17. Doesn't make hard cuts—easy to guard."

That player? Knight's own Hoosier standout, then freshman guard Steve Alford. Alford was one of the Big Ten's all-time great shooters and led IU in scoring in each of his four seasons. As adept and efficient at using screens as any player the Big Ten has seen in recent memory, Alford owned the school's all-time scoring record (2,438 points) before it was eclipsed by Calbert Cheaney in 1993.

It's important to note that Knight's comments didn't indicate a failed assessment of each player's abilities. Jordan and Ewing were both selected to the team and were first and third, respectively, on the team in scoring. The fourth leading scorer on that team was Alford, who averaged 10.3 points per contest.

Barkley, meanwhile, admitted he shouldn't have been named to the team because he was more focused on the start of his NBA career. Like Stockton, Barkley made the initial cuts and was in the final twenty before ultimately missing the team.

"That's the way it went [with Knight]," Garl says. "I may have sent a copy of those [notes] to Jordan, kind of a joke, to say hey, these were some notes Coach had on you."

★ ★ ★

The results of Knight's approach can't be disputed. Five of Team USA's eight wins were by at least 30 points, including a 96–65 win over Spain in the gold medal contest. Every win came by double digits as Knight's squad inserted itself as a formidable opponent to the 1960 Team USA squad (Jerry West, Walt Bellamy, Jerry Lucas, Oscar Robertson) in a discussion of the greatest amateur basketball teams the United States has ever assembled.

On a team littered with stars, there was no question that Michael Jordan (*right*) was the star on the 1984 US Olympic team. The 1984 National College Player of the Year from North Carolina, Jordan averaged a team-best 17.1 points per game.

Photo courtesy of Indiana University Archives.

That moniker wasn't a focus of Knight's, but he did focus on winning the gold medal once he was tabbed to lead the '84 team. "The thought of getting beat was unthinkable," Garl says. "Coach is such a patriot, and [former Vanderbilt Coach and Team USA assistant coach] C. M. [Newton], and the other coaches were similar in that regard. The thought of anything other than winning the gold never entered their heads."

While the United States' route to the gold medal wasn't necessarily considered a foregone conclusion before the Olympics got underway, the absence of one team was well noted. Following the US decision to boycott the 1980 Olympic Games in Moscow, the Soviet Union did the same in 1984. The Arvydas Sabonis–led team from the USSR was expected to be Team USA's stiffest competition in 1984 before the boycott.

But Knight wasn't about to let the absence of the Soviet squad lessen his team's accomplishment. And he wasn't shy about voicing his opinion on whether the Soviet team could have threatened his team for the gold medal. After all, Knight's Team USA squad had not only convincingly won the gold medal, but had also gone unbeaten in a series of exhibition

games against a number of NBA All-Star teams that included the likes of Larry Bird, Magic Johnson, and Isiah Thomas during their preparation for the Summer Olympics.

Long after the Olympics had concluded and Knight had returned to coaching the Hoosiers, the Soviet national team came to Bloomington for an exhibition contest. When Knight greeted Soviet national coach Alexander Gomelsky before the game, he had a gift—and some words—for the long-time coach. "Coach's gift to him was a pair of Air Jordan basketball shoes," Garl says. "And his remark to him was 'we would have beaten you anytime, anyplace with the 1984 team.'"

As Knight's gesture would suggest, that 1984 team was clearly led by Jordan, the 1984 Naismith College Basketball Player of the Year who averaged a team-best 17.1 points per game during the Olympic contests. His dominance was clear throughout the trials; a cumulative statistical sheet of the team's intrasquad games through July 6, 1984, showed Jordan easily led the team in field goals (176 field goals; Sam Perkins ranked second with 124) and field goal attempts (315; Perkins was second with 224) and his 38 steals ranked second only to Alvin Robertson's 53.

But as good as Jordan was, no one necessarily expected him to become the game's all-time best. His jump shot was considered by many to be a liability, and his college career had recently ended at the hands of, of all teams, Knight's Indiana squad. The Hoosiers held Jordan to 13 points in a 72–68 upset win over the top-ranked Tar Heels in the 1984 NCAA regional semifinals. "I don't think many were saying this was going to be the greatest player in the history of basketball," says Jim Butler, who in 1984 was an employee of WTTV-Channel 4 in Bloomington and the producer of the Bob Knight TV show.

Butler had been with Channel 4 since 1977, initially working as a cameraman on the Bob Knight show before becoming the producer of IU football coach Lee Corso's TV show in 1978. In 1984, the producer for the Bob Knight show left the TV station, and Butler moved into that role in the spring.

Knight's TV show aired throughout the Olympic trials, giving Butler an opportunity to witness the tryouts in Bloomington and to travel with the team for a series of games in California before the Olympics got underway. It was during one of those games that Butler said he saw Jordan do something that he can't necessarily describe, because he wasn't entirely sure of what he saw. "He made a play in one of those games that was almost indescribable—he drove the baseline,

Indiana basketball trainer Tim Garl (*left*) served in that same capacity for the 1984 US Olympic team, joining (*from left to right*) C. M. Newton, Don Donoher, George Raveling, and Bob Knight on Knight's hand-picked staff.

Photo courtesy of Indiana University Archives.

got trapped, was cut off," Butler said. "It then looked to me like he dematerialized on one side of the defender, and then rematerialized on the other side and then dunked.... I had never seen anything like that in my life. At that point I thought, this guy is going to be pretty good."

* * *

NBA teams agreed that Jordan had a chance to be special, which is why he decided to leave North Carolina after his junior season and declare for the 1984 NBA draft. The professional draft was held on June 19, just days before Knight made the final cuts to twelve players (from sixteen) for the US Olympic squad.

Today, the NBA draft is a spectacle. It airs on national television in primetime. Players, families, coaches, and friends are all in attendance, along with thousands of fans who have spent months debating whom their favorite NBA franchise should select and pay tens of millions of dollars.

That wasn't the case in 1984.

Virtually all of the draft-eligible players who remained at the US Olympic trials in Bloomington were expected to be selected early in the '84 draft (ultimately, eleven of the team's twelve players were first-round selections in either 1984 or 1985). But none of the '84 eligible players departed Bloomington for the event; instead they went through their regular routine in Bloomington prior to the draft, which took place at Madison Square Garden's Felt Forum.

The draft was broadcast by the USA Network, which arranged with WTTV to do a live feed from Bloomington as the participants in the trials were selected. Once they were drafted, they were led into the WTTV studio, where local television staff attached a microphone and fed questions to the players from the USA Network director in New York.

That afforded Butler another unforgettable memory, as he spent the afternoon and evening with those players while they waited to discover their NBA fate. "It was one of the best moments of my life," Butler said. "This took the whole afternoon to do, and after the first couple of interviews I left the studio and went to the [TV station's] lobby and just hung out with the guys.... At one point I'm there just hanging out talking with Michael Jordan, Leon Wood, guys like that. What a thrill."

By the time the first round had concluded, eight of the first eighteen selections had been players who remained in contention for a spot on the US Olympic squad—Jordan (selected third), Perkins (fourth), Robertson (seventh), Lancaster Gordon (eighth), Wood (tenth), Tim McCormick (twelfth), Jeff Turner (seventeenth) and Vern Fleming (eighteenth). A year later, five of the top seven picks in the 1985 NBA Draft were members of the '84 Olympic squad—Patrick Ewing (first), Wayman Tisdale (second), Jon Koncak (fifth), Joe Kleine (sixth) and Chris Mullin (seventh).

Butler remembers a couple of funny exchanges with Wood in the WTTV lobby as the '84 draft unfolded. Wood was selected by the Philadelphia 76ers, a team that had also taken US Olympic trial casualty Charles Barkley with the fifth overall pick. "Wood says, 'Oh man, I'm going to the 76ers, and that's where Charles is,'" Butler recalls. "'Charles is going to get all their money!'"

An outgoing personality from Cal State–Fullerton, Wood also poked some fun at Team USA teammate Vern Fleming, a point guard from Georgia whom Butler described as tremendously shy at the time. Fleming was taken eighteenth in the 1984 NBA Draft by the Indiana Pacers, who had gone an NBA-worst 26–56 in the 1983–84 season.

"Leon would say, 'Alvin [Robertson], where you going?' Oh, San Antonio," Butler recalls. "He'd ask all the other guys the same question.... Then he got to Vern. 'Vern, where you going? Indiana? Where? Oh, Vern. I'm sorry. I'm so sorry.'"

Ultimately, there was nothing for Wood to be sorry about—Fleming spent eleven of his twelve years in the NBA with the Pacers and still ranks among the franchise's all-time leaders in scoring (eighth), assists (second), steals (third), and games played (third). The Pacers advanced to the playoffs seven times during Fleming's career, including trips to the Eastern Conference Finals in each of his final two seasons in Indianapolis.

Wood, meanwhile, lasted only six years in the league, averaging 6.4 points for six different teams. He's now in his twenty-third year as an NBA referee.

* * *

By the time the 1984 NBA Draft had concluded and the players left the WTTV studio, eight of the sixteen players still under consideration for the US squad had their lives changing significantly. Jordan's initial contract included a $1 million signing bonus as part of a five-year, $6 million deal. Even the last of the US Olympic trials participants selected—Fleming—was set to earn $200,000 in his rookie season.

But according to Garl, Knight managed to keep the players' focus on Los Angeles and the quest for a gold medal. "Coach didn't deny [the draft] happened," Garl said. "But he said, 'Hey, you need to do the Olympic thing first. We have a job to do.'"

Knight's message was heard, and the team's focus didn't waver. Shortly after the NBA Draft, Knight cut the final four players—Lancaster Gordon, Johnny Dawkins, Chuck Person, and McCormick—on June 27 to get the roster down to the final twelve. From there, the team embarked on a coast-to-coast tour of exhibition games in preparation for the Olympics. Included was a July 9 matchup against NBA All-Stars at the Hoosier Dome in Indianapolis that drew 67,596 fans—a total that established a new record for the largest crowd to ever witness a basketball game.

"A game in July in the heat and humidity of summer draws 67,596 fans? Where else but Indiana?" says IU Assistant Athletic Director Chuck Crabb, who served as the public address announcer at the game and later as the Press Center interview manager at the Los Angeles games.

* * *

Team USA rolled through its competition once it arrived in Los Angeles. Robertson scored 18 to lead the team to a 48-point win over China in its opener. Jordan, Ewing, and Alford then led Team USA in scoring in the next three games as the squad continued to demolish its foes in group play, easily qualifying them for the medal round.

The team's quarterfinal opponent—West Germany—proved to be the stiffest competition during the Games, pushing Team USA before falling, 78–67. The West German team featured not only future NBA standout Detlef Schrempf, but also Hoosier junior Uwe Blab, who scored 10 points against Knight's US squad.

The biggest thing Team USA had to overcome in that game, though, wasn't Schrempf or Blab, but a bad tooth. Garl said that Jordan had been dealing with a toothache before the game, something they kept quiet. "I took him to the dentist and they worked on him a little bit and we went back to workouts, and afterwards he was still hurting," Garl said. "So I took him back and they ended up doing an extraction. So he had a tooth pulled before the game and didn't play that well (Jordan had 14 points and a game-high 6 turnovers). No one ever said anything about the tooth."

With the tooth gone and the West Germans dispatched, Team USA proceeded to whip Canada in the semifinals by 21 to set up a Gold Medal matchup with Spain.

On the court, there was little drama in the championship game, as Team USA cruised to a 96–65 win to claim the gold medal. The nervous moments, though, came before the game when the squad was warming up. "It's one of the great stories that people have probably never heard of," said Garl.

Throughout the games, Team USA's players and staff stayed in the Olympic village on the University of Southern California campus. Depending on traffic, the USC campus was a 20–30 minute drive from the men's basketball venue, the Forum in Inglewood.

As the team was warming up for the Gold Medal game, Garl noticed a problem—underneath his warmup, Jordan was wearing the wrong color uniform. Since the players dressed before heading over to the game, Jordan's white jersey was back in his room in the Olympic village.

The staff immediately sprang into action. Team USA assistant and Dayton University coach Don Donoher grabbed a sheriff's officer and the pair raced back to the USC campus. Garl, meanwhile, phoned the dormitory and told a close friend who was a member of the medical staff about the situation. Garl asked the trainer to get security to let him into Jordan's room to grab the white jersey. He would then hand it off to Donoher once he arrived.

That plan would have succeeded if not for one small issue. "I hadn't had a chance to tell Donoher they'd have the jersey in the lobby waiting for him," Garl said.

So the trainer and a security officer go into Jordan's room, get the jersey, and return to the lobby. Donoher, meanwhile, races through the lobby and up to Jordan's room. He tears through Jordan's belongings, unable to find the correct uniform.

Among the highlights for Indiana basketball fans in 1984 was a scrimmage game between Team USA and a squad of former Indiana University players. Among the former IU players to participate in that game were Quinn Buckner (*far left*) and Ray Tolbert (*background*), both of whom were playing in the NBA at the time.

Photo courtesy of Indiana University Archives.

As Donoher is searching for the jersey, the trainer with the jersey grew nervous, as he knew game time was approaching. "He ends up grabbing another officer and says, 'Hey, we got to go,'" Garl said. "'They have to have this to start the game.'" So the trainer and the second officer race through Los Angeles and Olympic traffic to the Forum, arriving in time for Jordan to switch uniforms before tip-off.

Soon afterward, Donoher returns and heads to Garl. "He's like, 'I searched everywhere, high and low, that jersey wasn't there,'" Garl said. "I said, 'Don, I'm sorry, we had it all set, you

Instead of holding the Team USA Olympic trials in Colorado Springs, Colorado, Bob Knight instead decided to bring seventy-three of the nation's premiere amateur basketball players to Bloomington as he went about the process of selecting twelve players to represent the country in the 1984 Olympics.

Photo courtesy of Indiana University Archives.

missed each other in the lobby, and they panicked and drove out here and we got it resolved.'"

That near miss did little to distract Jordan or the team before they took the court against Spain. In the final moments before the start if the gold medal game, Knight did what he traditionally did for all games—he began writing the offensive and defensive priorities on the locker room chalkboard. As he was writing Jordan interrupted his pregame ritual. "Jordan said, 'Coach, never mind this, we're ready to play,'" Garl recalls. "It's not necessary."

It wasn't—Jordan scored 20 points to lead Team USA to the 96–65 win.

* * *

It was a team that will forever hold its own among the great amateur basketball teams ever assembled. While there always would have been a special place in the hearts of Hoosiers for the squad thanks to the presence of Alford on the roster and Knight on the sidelines, the decision to hold the Olympic trials in Bloomington makes it even more special.

Garl indicated that was a decision Knight made, and it ran contrary to the norm of taking players to the US Olympic Committee headquarters in Colorado Springs, Colorado. But there was no pushback from USA Basketball. "The guys at the head of USA Basketball said it's your team, we don't want to present any obstacles or give you any problems," Garl said. "They didn't want anyone to have any regrets."

So with that decision cleared, seventy-three players and many of the nation's premier college coaches descended on

Bloomington in April of 1984. The players stayed at the IU Memorial Union, and Garl still has the original rooming list (one of the more interesting roommate tandems on the alphabetized list was Barkley and Alford). Among those who stayed at the Union was Garl, who offered up his house to members of the coaching staff to use. It created a very special environment in Bloomington, according to Crabb. "You had all of basketball's attention on Bloomington," Crabb said.

While the pursuit of the gold medal was the focus of both players and coaches during their stays in Bloomington, Knight didn't prevent the players from getting around town. The city was well-versed in the sport of college basketball, and the players were celebrities once they ventured away from the practice courts and mingled with the members of the community. "[The players] found Ye Old Regulator, they found Nick's," Crabb recalls. "They enjoyed what night life there is in Bloomington."

That was particularly true during off days. In an era long before cell phones, Garl recalls a time or two when he needed to find a player on an off day, but was unable to locate them in their Memorial Union hotel room. Left with no other options, he'd enlist a manager to track them down.

And where would they find the players?

"I'd send a manager down to Nick's, and more often than not, they could find some of the guys there," Garl said.

Proof of the players' presence remains to this day. At Nick's, several signed the wall in the hallway that leads to the "Hump" room on the establishment's top floor. Among those players was Joe Kleine, who included this saying with his signature: "If the beer's cold, we'll win the gold."

While the players bounced around town when the opportunity presented itself, the coaching staff followed Knight's lead and were rarely seen around town. When the coaching staff headed out to eat, they'd often go to a private dining area in a back room of Smitty's, a long-since-departed local dining establishment on the corner of Walnut Street and Hillside Drive that Knight often frequented. "They'd eat every southern Indiana fat food delicacy there was and just have a ball," Crabb said.

The coaches also spent many long hours in and around Assembly Hall and the IU fieldhouse, which was the headquarters during the early part of the trials in April when all seventy-three players remained. With ten courts set up inside the fieldhouse, Knight and other coaches sat atop a forklift where they could watch all of the games from one location.

When the day's games would end, the staff would retreat to the IU locker room to discuss which players would make up the US squad. In that locker room, Garl said, was a new state-of-the-art side-by-side refrigerator donated by one of Bloomington's biggest employers at the time, RCA. Making sure things were in it, meanwhile, was the duty of former IU basketball manager Steve Skoronski. "Steve's major responsibility was to make sure the right kind of beer was in the fridge," Garl said. "He had to make sure he had a little bit of everything because you had so many coaches. They didn't all drink beer, but Steve had to make sure if someone wanted something in particular that it was there, otherwise he was running to Big Red to go get it."

When Garl ventured into the locker room during those coaches' sessions, he remembers it was a Who's Who of big names in the college game. In addition to Knight, Donoher, and Newton, there were George Raveling, Gene Keady, Mike Krzyzewski, Digger Phelps, Henry Iba, and Pete Newell, who were among the coaching legends or legends-to-be that were sharing their thoughts and bantering back and forth. "They all took it seriously, but I also remember a lot of laughing and a lot of storytelling," Garl said. "I'm sure if you'd ask any of them they'd remember that time very fondly, having a lot of peers together like that."

That group of coaches, led by Knight, assembled a team that basketball fans remember fondly as well, one that cemented itself as one of the country's all-time best on the amateur level.

And how could they not? After all, it had a scoring machine in Jordan who would go on to win ten NBA scoring titles.

"Poor spacing—stays next to man," Knight commented about Jordan.

And the team had a defensive stopper in the backcourt in Alvin Robertson, a standout at Arkansas who would go on to win NBA Defensive Player of the Year honors in his second year in the league and still owns the NBA record for most steals per game in a career.

"Poor stance, gets turned on screen, loses track of the ball and man," Knight wrote.

Offensively, Chris Mullin was a versatile inside-outside forward who was a three-time Big East Conference Player of the Year and ended up playing for sixteen years in the NBA.

"Does not get set to shoot, could use a shot fake."

Coach Bob Knight and the US Olympic coaching staff kept cumulative statistics for the trials participants throughout the selection process. This July 6, 1984, statistics sheet includes the scrimmage totals for the twelve players who made the final June 27 cut, along with the team's two alternates (Chuck Person and Johnny Dawkins).

Photo courtesy of Indiana University Archives.

And in the post, the team had Ewing, arguably the most intimidating defensive defender the college game has seen in the last forty years.

"Doesn't take away step into lane—no blockout," Knight wrote.

Who could find anything wrong with that team?

DATE: 2-6-84 OFFENSE: Totals + Date

WHITE	FG	FGA	OFF REB		DEF REB	STEALS	TURN-OVERS	ASSISTS	POST FEED
Alford	68	127	9	94	23	26	34	56	58
Dawkins	42	73	5	20	21	37	43	57	14
Ewing	99	184	37	81	54	13	45	17	7
Fleming	64	119	11	51	40	29	37	59	18
Jordan	176	315	30	66	86	38	32	210	28
Kerine	58	127	34	14	55	20	34	22	11
Koncak	62	121	30	81	58	10	30	18	2
Mullin	119	221	15	60	27	26	38	67	96
Perkins	124	226	34	76	58	29	31	30	17
Person	66	135	16	61	42	11	22	14	22
TOTALS									

BLUE	FG	FGA	OFF REB		DEF REB	STEALS	TURN-OVERS	ASSISTS	POST FEED
Robertson	71	192	26	63	43	53	74	79	36
Tisdale	94	131	30	14	99	10	35	54	19
Turner	48	74	22	12	60	10	39	39	35
Wood	50	101	6	29	23	29	67	92	24

JOHN C. DECKER has nearly thirty years of experience in and around IU Athletics. He spent fifteen years covering the Hoosiers for a series of sports publications, including *Inside Indiana* magazine.

PETE DIPRIMIO is an award-winning sportswriter and author. He's won more than forty national and Indiana state writing awards and has had more than two dozen children's books published.

DOUG WILSON is a Bloomington native who worked as a reporter at the *Bloomington Herald-Times* for ten years, serving as sports editor during his last three years there.